THE HONOURABLE
COMPANY OF
EDINBURGH GOLFERS
MUIRFIELD

Practice Ground

CARD OF THE CHAMPIONSHIP COURSE

Hole	Yards	Par	Hole	Yards	Par
1	447	4	10	475	4
2	351	4	11	385	4
3	379	4	12	381	4
4	180	3	13	159	3
5	559	5	14	449	4
6	469	4	15	417	4
7	185	3	16	188	3
8	444	4	17	550	5
9	504	5	18	448	4
OUT	3518	36	IN	3452	35
			OUT	3518	36
			TOTAL	6970	71

THE OPEN
CHAMPIONSHIP
1992

PRESENTED IN ASSOCIATION WITH

1992 Open champion Nick Faldo with wife, Gill, and caddie, Fanny **Sunesson**.

THE OPEN CHAMPIONSHIP 1992

WRITERS
ROBERT SOMMERS
RAYMOND JACOBS
MICHAEL MCDONNELL
MICHAEL WILLIAMS
MARINO PARASCENZO
ALISTER NICOL
JOHN HOPKINS

PHOTOGRAPHERS
LAWRENCE LEVY
MICHAEL COHEN

EDITOR
BEV NORWOOD

AUTHORISED BY THE
CHAMPIONSHIP COMMITTEE
OF THE ROYAL AND ANCIENT
GOLF CLUB OF ST ANDREWS

TRANSWORLD PUBLISHERS LTD
61-63 Uxbridge Road, London W5 5SA

TRANSWORLD PUBLISHERS (AUSTRALIA) PTY LTD
15-23 Helles Avenue, Moorebank, NSW 2170

TRANSWORLD PUBLISHERS (NZ) LTD
Cnr Moselle and Waipareira Aves,
Henderson, Auckland

Published 1992 by Partridge Press
a division of Transworld Publishers Ltd
Copyright © 1992 The Championship Committee Merchandising
Limited

Statistics of 121st Open Championship produced on a
Unisys Computer System

Photographs on pp. 17-21, 88 courtesy of Brian Morgan
Photographs on pp. 14-15, 36, 53, 62, 70, 73, 82 courtesy of Danielle Fluer

A CIP catalogue record for this book is available
from the British Library

1 85225 1867

Typeset by Davis Design
Printed in Great Britain
by Bath Colourbooks Ltd

CONTENTS

INTRODUCTION by R. H. Evans, C. B. E.   7

THE CHAMPIONSHIP COMMITTEE   8

INTRODUCTION by W. G. N. Roach   9

FOREWORD by Nick Faldo   11

121st OPEN CHAMPIONSHIP   12

ROUND MUIRFIELD   16

THE VENUE: 100 YEARS OF OPENS AT MUIRFIELD by Raymond Jacobs   17

RETROSPECTIVE: THE LEGACY OF GARY PLAYER by Michael McDonnell   23

DAY 1: PATE, FLOYD START WITH 64s by Robert Sommers   27

COMMENTARY: AT AGE 49, FLOYD DRIVES ON by Michael Williams   39

DAY 2: FALDO SETS 36-HOLE RECORD by Robert Sommers   43

COMMENTARY: WHERE HAVE FAVOURITES GONE? by Marino Parascenzo   55

DAY 3: IT'S FALDO'S — TO WIN OR LOSE by Robert Sommers   59

COMMENTARY: THREE ON VERGE OF SUCCESS by Alister Nicol   71

DAY 4: THE BEST GOLFER OF HIS TIME? by Robert Sommers   75

COMMENTARY: A VICTORY WORTH CRYING ABOUT by John Hopkins   89

RECORDS OF THE OPEN CHAMPIONSHIP   95

PAST RESULTS   100

FINAL RESULTS   109

INTRODUCTION

BY R. H. EVANS, C. B. E.
Chief Executive
British Aerospace plc

British Aerospace, a world force in the Aircraft and Motor Vehicle industry, uses the British Open Golf Championship as the flagship occasion for its business entertaining because it provides the opportunity for meeting our international and British customers in an exceptional atmosphere as well as in most comfortable and elegant surroundings.

We are delighted and proud to be thus associated with the premier golf tournament in the world and look forward to the 1993 Championship which will be held on the Kentish coastline at the Royal St. George's Golf Club, one of England's classic links courses.

R. H. Evans, C. B. E.

THE CHAMPIONSHIP COMMITTEE

CHAIRMAN

W. G. N. ROACH

DEPUTY CHAIRMAN

J. C. DAWSON

COMMITTEE

M. VANS AGNEW
A. R. COLE-HAMILTON
R. M. E. DAVITT
P. W. J. GREENHOUGH
R. H. PALMER
D. I. PEPPER
P. M. G. UNSWORTH
W. J. UZIELLI
R. P. WHITE
R. S. WHITMORE

BUSINESS SUB-COMMITTEE CHAIRMAN

H. M. CAMPBELL

RULES SUB-COMMITTEE CHAIRMAN

J. L. S. PASQUILL

ADDITIONAL MEMBER

J. R. VAUGHAN-EVANS
COUNCIL OF NATIONAL GOLF UNIONS

SECRETARY

M. F. BONALLACK, OBE

DEPUTY SECRETARY

W. G. WILSON

CHAMPIONSHIP SECRETARY

D. HILL

ASSISTANT SECRETARY (CHAMPIONSHIPS)

D. R. WEIR

INTRODUCTION

BY W. G. N. ROACH
Chairman of Championship Committee
Royal and Ancient Golf Club of St Andrews

After the cold, wind and rain we experienced at Muirfield in 1987, the weather for the 121st Open Championship was excellent apart from some squally rain on the last afternoon and, at times, the lack of a really stiff wind to test the golfers.

The standard of play by the 156 competitors at the home of the Honourable Company of Edinburgh Golfers was outstanding and Nick Faldo's 272 aggregate matched the fifth lowest in Open Championship history while John Cook's 273 was the second best ever by a runner-up.

Our champion further established his credentials among the best golfers of all time with his third Open Championship and his second at Muirfield, an accomplishment matched only by James Braid (1901, 1906) in the time of the Great Triumvirate.

This year's Open Championship marked 100 years since the Open was first played at Muirfield and the Championship Committee are grateful to the Honourable Company of Edinburgh Golfers for the courtesy of their course. We would also like to thank the many hundreds of volunteers for their help during the week.

We appreciate the support of British Aerospace in the publication of this official record of the 121st Open Championship. We believe this annual book will be a worthy memento of the occasion, and in that regard we thank the writers and photographers whose work is represented here.

W. G. N. Roach

FOREWORD

BY NICK FALDO

Even now, almost a week after the event, I feel the emotion as I think about the 1992 Open Championship at Muirfield. When you set your heart on the major championships and win as I did — playing your best golf at the time you needed it most — all sorts of feelings come rushing forth. You cry and laugh; you are exhilarated and exhausted.

The support of my close friends and family, especially my wife, Gill, has been important in all my victories, and this time, more than any other, I also drew strength from the tremendous number of spectators encouraging me on, even when it seemed that my prospects for victory were dim indeed.

So once again, here's to the marvellous galleries at Muirfield!

You never grow tired of victory. Each time I win, I am all the more determined to keep my golf career on line and hopefully to add to my victory total. I want to know that I have done my best and that my shortcomings are not for a lack of preparation or effort.

Annual books such as the Open Championship series are wonderful reminders of times past, for golfers and spectators alike. I hope that you will enjoy recalling the week at Muirfield as much as I will.

Nick Faldo

121ST OPEN CHAMPIONSHIP

*Denotes amateurs

NAME	SCORES				TOTAL	MONEY
Nick Faldo, England	66	64	69	73	272	£95,000
John Cook, USA	66	67	70	70	273	75,000
Jose Maria Olazabal, Spain	70	67	69	68	274	64,000
Steve Pate, USA	64	70	69	73	276	53,000
Andrew Magee, USA	67	72	70	70	279	30,071
Malcolm Mackenzie, England	71	67	70	71	279	30,071
Robert Karlsson, Sweden	70	68	70	71	279	30,071
Ian Woosnam, Wales	65	73	70	71	279	30,071
Gordon Brand, Jr., Scotland	65	68	72	74	279	30,071
Donnie Hammond, USA	70	65	70	74	279	30,071
Ernie Els, South Africa	66	69	70	74	279	30,071
Mark O'Meara, USA	71	68	72	69	280	17,383
James Spence, England	71	68	70	71	280	17,383
Raymond Floyd, USA	64	71	73	72	280	17,383
Sandy Lyle, Scotland	68	70	70	72	280	17,383
Larry Rinker, USA	69	68	70	73	280	17,383
Chip Beck, USA	71	68	67	74	280	17,383
Greg Norman, Australia	71	72	70	68	281	13,200
Ian Baker-Finch, Australia	71	71	72	68	282	11,066
Tom Kite, USA	70	69	71	72	282	11,066
Hale Irwin, USA	70	73	67	72	282	11,066
Tom Purtzer, USA	68	69	75	71	283	8,950
Peter Mitchell, England	69	71	72	71	283	8,950
Paul Lawrie, Scotland	70	72	68	73	283	8,950
Duffy Waldorf, USA	69	70	73	72	284	7,700
Billy Andrade, USA	69	71	70	74	284	7,700
Peter Senior, Australia	70	69	70	75	284	7,700
Craig Parry, Australia	67	71	76	71	285	6,658
Jodie Mudd, USA	71	69	74	71	285	6,658
Mark Calcavecchia, USA	69	71	73	72	285	6,658
Russ Cochran, USA	71	68	72	74	285	6,658
Mats Lanner, Sweden	72	68	71	74	285	6,658
Mark McNulty, Zimbabwe	71	70	70	74	285	6,658
Tony Johnstone, Zimbabwe	72	71	74	69	286	5,760
Corey Pavin, USA	69	74	73	70	286	5,760
Payne Stewart, USA	70	73	71	72	286	5,760
Steve Elkington, Australia	68	70	75	73	286	5,760
Anders Forsbrand, Sweden	70	72	70	74	286	5,760
Ronan Rafferty, N. Ireland	69	71	75	72	287	5,083
Steven Richardson, England	74	68	73	72	287	5,083
Lee Trevino, USA	69	71	73	74	287	5,083
Wayne Grady, Australia	73	69	71	74	287	5,083
De Wet Basson, South Africa	71	71	71	74	287	5,083
Lee Janzen, USA	66	73	73	75	287	5,083
Mike Harwood, Australia	72	68	76	72	288	4,675
Jose Coceres, Argentina	74	69	73	72	288	4,675
Rocco Mediate, USA	67	75	73	73	288	4,675
Craig Mann, Australia	74	69	72	73	288	4,675
Brian Marchbank, Scotland	71	72	71	74	288	4,675
Lanny Wadkins, USA	69	69	75	75	288	4,675

Vijay Singh, Fiji	69	72	76	72	289	4,075
Roger Mackay, Australia	73	70	73	73	289	4,075
Nick Price, Zimbabwe	69	73	73	74	289	4,075
Barry Lane, England	73	69	73	74	289	4,075
Orrin Vincent, USA	67	75	77	71	290	3,875
Costantino Rocca, Italy	67	75	73	75	290	3,875
Mark Brooks, USA	71	71	73	75	290	3,875
David Feherty, N. Ireland	71	70	72	77	290	3,875
Bernhard Langer, Germany	70	72	76	73	291	3,650
Wayne Riley, Australia	71	72	75	73	291	3,650
Michael Clayton, Australia	72	70	75	74	291	3,650
Paul Azinger, USA	70	69	75	77	291	3,650
William Guy, Scotland	72	71	70	78	291	3,650
Danny Mijovic, Canada	70	71	80	71	292	3,425
Hendrik Buhrmann, South Africa	70	72	75	75	292	3,425
Craig Stadler, USA	72	70	75	75	292	3,425
Roger Chapman, England	72	71	71	78	292	3,425
Jon Robson, England	70	71	78	74	293	3,237
Per-Ulrik Johansson, Sweden	67	74	77	75	293	3,237
Peter O'Malley, Australia	72	70	76	75	293	3,237
* Daren Lee, England	68	72	77	76	293	
Andrew Sherborne, England	72	69	75	77	293	3,237
Fred Funk, USA	71	71	76	76	294	3,200
Paul Mayo, Wales	70	72	79	74	295	3,200
John Daly, USA	74	69	80	75	298	3,200

NON QUALIFIERS AFTER 36 HOLES
(All professionals receive £600)

Ian Palmer, South Africa	73 71	144
Bob Tway, USA	71 73	144
Jim Gallagher, Jr., USA	74 70	144
Jeff Sluman, USA	70 74	144
Gary Evans, England	71 73	144
Stephen Bennett, England	69 75	144
Jeremy Robinson, England	71 73	144
Mark Roe, England	73 71	144
Howard Clark, England	74 70	144
Tommy Nakajima, Japan	72 72	144
Billy Ray Brown, USA	69 75	144
David Gilford, England	70 74	144
Larry Mize, USA	68 76	144
Keith Waters, England	74 70	144
John McHenry, Ireland	72 72	144
Tom Weiskopf, USA	74 71	145
Paul Broadhurst, England	75 70	145
Rodger Davis, Australia	71 74	145
Paul McGinley, Ireland	76 69	145
Paul Way, England	74 71	145
Kenneth Walker, Scotland	75 70	145
* Stephen Pullan, England	74 71	145
Jeff Maggert, USA	68 77	145
Seve Ballesteros, Spain	70 75	145
Sam Torrance, Scotland	73 72	145
Philip Walton, Ireland	71 74	145
Ian Spencer, England	76 70	146

Gary Player, South Africa	71 75	146
Colin Montgomerie, Scotland	76 70	146
Tony Charnley, England	74 72	146
Craig McLellan, Scotland	72 74	146
Freddy George, England	75 71	146
Mark James, England	70 76	146
Greg Turner, New Zealand	70 76	146
Philip Harrison, England	75 71	146
Jose Maria Canizares, Spain	72 75	147
Richard Boxall, England	73 74	147
Curtis Strange, USA	74 73	147
Phillip Price, Wales	75 72	147
Paul Moloney, Australia	74 73	147
Andrew Hare, England	73 74	147
Des Smyth, Ireland	72 75	147
Jim Payne, England	71 76	147
Eduardo Romero, Argentina	71 77	148
Fred Couples, USA	70 78	148
Naomichi Ozaki, Japan	72 76	148
Darren Clarke, Ireland	76 72	148
Tom Watson, USA	73 75	148
Jack Nicklaus, USA	75 73	148
David Williams, England	74 74	148
Nils Lindeblad, Sweden	69 79	148
Neal Briggs, England	72 77	149
Magnus Sunesson, Sweden	74 75	149
Keith Clearwater, USA	74 75	149
Chris Gray, Australia	73 76	149
David Eddiford, England	74 75	149

Justin Hobday, Zimbabwe	75 74	149
Jose Rivero, Spain	72 77	149
Johan Rystrom, Sweden	75 74	149
Michael Archer, England	74 75	149
Paul Wesselingh, England	75 74	149
Eric Giraud, France	78 72	150
Masashi Ozaki, Japan	74 76	150
Davis Love III, USA	73 77	150
Marcus Knight, England	79 71	150
* Michael Welch, England	76 74	150
Mike McLean, England	73 77	150
Kevin Jones, Wales	69 81	150
* Mitch Voges, USA	71 79	150
Ken Trimble, Australia	75 76	151
Mark Davis, England	76 75	151
Mark Mouland, Wales	73 78	151
Gary Emerson, England	75 76	151
Andrew Coltart, Scotland	76 76	152
Gary Torbett, England	78 74	152
* Guy Wolstenholme, England	77 76	153
Dave Padgett, England	76 77	153
Todd Hamilton, USA	76 78	154
Colin Brooks, Scotland	77 78	155
Christian Post, Denmark	79 79	158
John Hay, England	79 79	158

The Honourable Company of Edinburgh Golfers, as Nick Faldo prepares to putt for the 121st Open Championship.

ROUND MUIRFIELD

No. 1 447 Yards, Par 4

The drive must be held on a narrow target between a long snaking bunker on the left and rough opposite. Into the prevailing wind, as it sweeps in from Gullane Hill, a long iron, or even a wood, will be needed for the second shot. Potentially one of the most rigorous introductions in British championship golf.

No. 2 351 Yards, Par 4

Although in 1987 this hole and the next ranked respectively 11th and seventh in degree of difficulty, they clearly offer birdie opportunities. To access the approach to a long and wide green carrying awkward borrows, the tee shot should be, so to speak, off the wall, which runs along the left side and, of course, is out of bounds.

No. 3 379 Yards, Par 4

The preferred line from the tee is to the left for the best approach to the green, tucked as it is between two sandhills. This is the first of three holes in succession running in the same direction.

No. 4 180 Yards, Par 3

Like its three companion short holes, the elevated green here slopes from back to front. The cardinal rule is to be up so as to avoid the forward bunkering, the mound to the right and the steep fall of ground to the left.

No. 5 559 Yards, Par 5

A progression of bunkers on the right of the fairway, out of view from the tee behind a ridge, again requires the drive to favour the left side. There are more bunkers on the approach to a green with an unusual variety of levels. Johnny Miller eliminated all the problems in the second round in 1972 when he holed his three-wood second shot.

No. 6 469 Yards, Par 4

This hole has a slight dog-leg left and has been identified by Jack Nicklaus as being the most awkward tee shot on the course. The four bunkers — two visible, two not so over a ridge — on the left of a split-level fairway determine that for a fair view of the green the drive should be to the right.

No. 7 185 Yards, Par 3

Comparable in design to No. 4, this one faces into the prevailing wind. Three bunkers to the left and one to the right await the misdirected tee shot. Depending on the wind's strength and its direction, a difference of two or three clubs could be dictated.

No. 8 444 Yards, Par 4

The cluster of no fewer than seven bunkers on the right of the fairway (which Walter Hagen used to avoid by driving farther to the right still onto rough ground where a copse now lies) demands the opposite route from the tee. The approach is partially blind over cross bunkers, beyond which there is about 30 yards of dead ground in front of the green.

No. 9 504 Yards, Par 5

This is one of the most exacting holes in all of championship golf. Downwind, it can be reached in two; more probably playing into the wind, two solid shots are needed to offer any hope of an approach close enough to the hole on a green of complex borrows to make a birdie. The wall to the left and the bunkers to the right have to be negotiated with the greatest of care.

No. 10 475 Yards, Par 4

In a left-hand wind (the predominant one), the two bunkers on the right of the fairway become particularly dangerous to the tee shot. The distances achieved these days mean that the two deep cross bunkers are probably less exacting as hazards than the green's sharp right-to-left slope.

No. 11 385 Yards, Par 4

Those untroubled by the blind tee shot, the fairway cunningly bunkered, and the heavily guarded, steeply sloping green may have the time to appreciate the best, if distant, views of Edinburgh, the Forth bridges, and the coast and hills of Fife.

No. 12 381 Yards, Par 4

This is a hole of deceptive difficulty, especially if it is played into the prevailing wind. The fairway is well-bunkered and flanked by rough to demand an accurate drive down the hill. It is neither advisable to be too far left from the tee or too far right with the approach to a long green constricted at its entrance.

No. 13 159 Yards, Par 3

The depth of the bunkers patrolling both sides of the green — long, narrow, and steeply raked from the rear — makes this one of Open golf's most exacting short holes. To finish above the hole, moreover, leaves a downhill putt of inhibiting slickness.

No. 14 449 Yards, Par 4

Anyone who makes four 4s during the championship will consider he has achieved something exceptional. Although the entrance to the green is generous enough, the landing area from the tee is not, located between three bunkers on the left, the preferred side, and one to the right. As the hole again faces the regular wind, it is no one's idea of an easy mark.

No. 15 417 Yards, Par 4

Continuing in approximately its predecessor's direction, the key shot on this hole is the drive, which must avoid the flanking bunkers. Even then, the camel-backed green makes the approach shot difficult to stop close enough to the hole to provide a good opportunity for a birdie.

No. 16 188 Yards, Par 3

This is the longest of the four short holes and the third of them to face down the normal wind. Heavily guarded by bunkers and rough, the green can only be safely boarded with the most accurate of shots. The slope, again steep, tends to drag the ball towards the left-hand bunkers, although it was from one opposite that Lee Trevino holed out on his way to winning in 1972.

No. 17 550 Yards, Par 5

As the 71st, this hole had a huge influence in deciding two of the last three Opens at Muirfield. In 1972 and 1987, Trevino and Paul Azinger both drove into a bunker, but whereas Trevino holed for a chip for par to edge ahead of Tony Jacklin, who pitched short and took three putts, Azinger bogeyed and Nick Faldo soon had his first title.

No. 18 448 Yards, Par 4

Jacklin and Azinger also found this sting in the course's tail sharp and destructive. Needing 4s to be sure of victory, both Nicklaus, in 1966, and Trevino found the solution by avoiding the strategically placed fairway and greenside bunkers.

100 YEARS OF OPENS AT MUIRFIELD

BY RAYMOND JACOBS

What would they make of the game now, those intrepid members of the Company of Gentlemen Golfers, if they were discussing its development at Luckie Clephan's tavern in Leith, the first headquarters of what was to become the Honourable Company of Edinburgh Golfers? As they set about taking on board a cargo of claret, estimated in one account to be sometimes as much as 'the best part of a gallon,' they could not then have even imagined the evolution of clubs and balls, the growth of courses and the hugely improved conditions, the higher standards of clubhouses, and the explosion in the number of players. The economics of the game, whether in prize money for professionals, provision of opportunities for amateurs, or the expansion in sales of clothing and equipment, also would be far beyond their modest horizons.

All the same, it has been confirmed by documentary evidence that the Honourable Company is the world's oldest golf club. On 7 March 1744, Edinburgh Town Council responded to the latest of several applications for formal recognition made by 'several Gentlemen of Honour, skillfull in the ancient and healthfull exercise of the Golf,' although the stipulation was prudently included that 'upon no pretence whatsoever the City of Edinburgh shall be put to any sort of expense in playing for the same Club.' The winner was to be styled 'Captain of the Golf,' who, in surely a unique,

Home of the Honourable Company.

if dubious distinction in sport for a player, also was given the responsibility for settling all disputes regarding the golf and golfers.

Subsequently the need for formal playing regulations became obvious, and the game's first set of rules, numbering 13 and known as the Leith Code, were devised. Ten years later the same rules were adopted by the group of golfers at St Andrews whose activities would eventually lead to the formation of the Royal and Ancient Golf Club. In 1768 the tavern life was abandoned for a golf house, the club's competitions continuing, however, on the links, which consisted of five holes, all around 400 yards long. Overcrowding, poor drainage and military training during the Napoleonic Wars gradually began to convince the members that a move to Musselburgh would have to be undertaken. Financial problems were another complication and, in 1836, the club finally severed its long connection with Leith.

By the time another 40 years had passed, no fewer than four clubs had premises at Musselburgh, Royal Burgess and Bruntsfield Links having joined Royal Musselburgh and the Honourable Company. Congestion again dictated a search for new pastures and, by coincidence, the site of one racecourse was exchanged for another, outside Gullane on land known as Hundred Acre Field, where the annual East Lothian races were held.

The 12th hole, 381 yards and par 4, is known to be deceptively difficult.

Three bunkers to the left and one to the right await misdirected tee shots at No. 7.

Muirfield, initially restricted to 16 holes, although not for long, opened for play on 3 May 1891, and within a single year the course was judged ready to be host to the first of its 14 Open Championships to date, despite Andrew Kirkaldy's sarcastic remark that Old Tom Morris' design was 'just an auld watter meedie.' The Honourable Company had begun a new chapter of their remarkable history.

The Open's almost instantaneous appearance at Muirfield becomes perhaps less surprising when it is recalled that the club had in 1871 linked with Prestwick, the founders, and the Royal and Ancient to run the championship and provide a trophy after Young Tom Morris had made the Belt his own with three successive victories. From 1872 the championship rotated among these clubs, and so when the Honourable Company left Musselburgh, the Open duly followed. Adverse opinions about the quality and character of the course were doubtless unalleviated by the victory of Harold Hilton, not only an amateur but an Englishman to boot, who also was the first to win the title over 72 holes, then constricted into two days.

It is worth recording at this point Muirfield's un-equalled association with innovative developments

in the Open. In 1896 Harry Vardon beat J. H. Taylor in the first 36-hole play-off, and five years later James Braid won the first of his five titles. In 1912 Ted Ray gained his first, and only, victory, as did Alf Perry in 1935. In 1959 Gary Player won the first of his three championships, as did Jack Nicklaus in 1966, when the Open was first extended from three days to four, and the prize fund was increased after the championship had started. Lee Trevino in 1972 became the first since Arnold Palmer, a decade before, to retain the title, and 10 years later Tom Watson won the third of his five titles in the first championship to finish on Sunday. By then, though, radical changes to the course had long since been made.

The motivation for undertaking alterations came very soon after the opening of the original course — the need for a longer test to accommodate golf ball developments. Nothing much changes, it seems. Braid's reduction of his winning total of 309 in 1901 by nine strokes only five years later was bound to have been assisted by the replacement in 1902 of the gutta percha ball with the Haskell ball. And so the course, which in 1896 had been extended by more than 600 yards to 6,194 yards, was lengthened fur-

The 17th hole, a par 5 of 550 yards, has a history of deciding Open Championships.

ther by the acquisition of additional land so that by 1919, at 6,501 yards, it was around 1,000 yards longer than the first layout. More land still was bought in the early 1920s, and the celebrated English architect, Harry Colt, was brought in to produce the design which is essentially the course so highly regarded today.

The outward half moves more or less clockwise and the inward half in the opposite direction, with no more than three consecutive holes — the third to the fifth — playing in the same direction. Since the wind can change tack almost as frequently as the course, the golfer's club judgement and his ability to adapt to these fluctuations are constantly called to account, especially in avoiding bunkers of exceptional depth — and described by Nicklaus after his first sight of them as the most fastidiously built he had ever seen. Henry Cotton, as shrewd an observer as there has been, won the last of his three Opens at Muirfield in 1948, doubtless encouraging him to deliver his judgement that the course was 'always in perfect condition and cruelly fair.'

Whatever the opinion of the courses might have been as they evolved over the years, the survivor's place in the pantheon of the game is assured and reinforced by the renown of the players who have won the Open at Muirfield — Hilton, Vardon, Braid twice, Walter Hagen, Cotton, Player, Nicklaus, Trevino, and Watson. The exceptions were Ray, one of only five players to intervene when, from 1894 until 1914, the Great Triumvirate of Vardon, Braid and Taylor won the championship 16 times in 21 attempts, and Perry. Ray — strong, bucolic and unorthodox — was sneeringly described as 'that animated clod-stamper,' but in 1920, he further showed his mettle by winning the US Open, a feat not achieved again by another British professional until 50 years later, by Tony Jacklin. Perry was self-effacing to the point of invisibility, but proved himself no less deserving.

Their victories must have warmed the hearts of all those who enjoy the occasional deflation of the great and the good at the hands of the other ranks. Ray, for example, had tremendous powers of recovery from the rough, an attribute much appreciated by the newspaper cartoonists of the day. Perry had a 'slashing, round-the-corner swing, with the right hand held well under the grip, knuckles to the ground,' Bernard Darwin observed. 'He pitches and putts with the almost insolent confidence of a small boy with his master's iron on a caddie's miniature course.' On the other hand, Hagen at Muirfield won the last of his four Opens in only eight attempts, and Cotton's third was established by a record score of

66 in the second round, with King George VI among the appreciative audience.

The last sight of Perry after his four-stroke victory over Alf Padgham was at Drem Station, waiting alone with his clubs and travelling bag for the train south, and 35 years later he politely, but firmly, declined his invitation to the first champions' dinner hosted at St Andrews by the Royal and Ancient. The others were, to say the least, not short of flamboyance or dominance and, indeed, were usually able triumphantly to combine the two. Player won in spite of making a double bogey at the 72nd hole and Trevino cruelly thwarted Jacklin in 1972. Nicklaus, who finished second, was rightly or wrongly judged to have played too defensively for the first three rounds to add the championship to the Masters and Open titles he had already won that year, and go on to try to complete the professional Grand Slam with the USPGA championship.

Muirfield's association with golf on an international level has not, of course, been confined to the Open Championship. Two Walker Cup and Curtis Cup matches have been played over what has been described as a course which absolves the players from guesswork, so clearly are the targets defined from the tee to the green. Conditions were so benign in 1980, though, that Watson and Horacio Carbonetti, of Argentina, shot 64 and Isao Aoki, the Japanese professional, 63, which he shares with four others as the Open Championship record. These were scores which made even more prehistoric the round of 79 (48-31) returned by a member in the club's spring meeting of 1894, a major factor in the decision later taken to strengthen the challenge of the original course.

The official historian, George Pottinger, wrote that Muirfield 'has always had the reputation for being, perhaps more than any other, a club which likes to keep itself to itself.' If so, its office-bearers have kept a weather-eye open, too, on their responsibilities as curators of a magnificent golfing inheritance. And, as one captain unabashedly noted, 'from pure self-interest and on financial grounds alone we must keep in the front rank.' To that end, apart from the Open Championship and the other events mentioned, the club has been host to the one Ryder Cup match played in Scotland, in 1973, and amateur competitions also have been accommodated, including six British and Scottish championships and the Home Internationals, on four occasions.

If the paradox of the Honourable Company of Edinburgh Golfers is that they seem positively to enjoy flaunting their exclusivity, then that is also surely the prerogative of any private club, sporting or otherwise. As it is, the members are to be envied their course and their lunch table, equally renowned for its excellence by those who have been fortunate enough to experience both. The membership of every club on the Open Championship rota is sure to be divided on the effect on their own golfing enjoyment of a regular invasion which lasts up to four months. The other side of the argument could be that they appreciate their possession all the more when it is returned to them.

There are numerous bunkers at No. 8, 444 yards and par 4.

Gary Player transformed golf by naked ambition — he wanted to win and was not ashamed to show it.

THE LEGACY OF GARY PLAYER

BY MICHAEL McDONNELL

The ultimate tribute to the life and times of a great man is that he receives his own imperishable place in history for having played a role for which his name will always be remembered.

In golfing terms, such recognition amounts to more than just a colossal tally of victories which symbolize a personal supremacy and excellence by which future generations can judge themselves.

Victories are important, of course, but invariably destined to be overtaken and capped in the fullness of time. There is, however, a different, more permanent kind of distinction which is locked safely in the chronological evolution of the game and therefore can never be threatened.

This then is the manner in which the phenomenon of Gary Player is to be regarded and remembered, because the archives will show that this diminutive South African transformed the traditional concept of the game — or rather the playing of it — so that it was never quite the same again.

It was not, he concluded, merely a pastime in which a natural flair and eye for a ball were the only requirements, and that the best preparation — if any were really needed — was the game itself.

Player held a different view. He perceived it as pure athletics — albeit mechanical in form — but, as such, requiring a regimen of personal training, development, discipline and diet that would be afforded to any other pursuit.

It was not so much dogma, as discovery. And while it was greeted at first with mild ridicule, it produced another, even greater impact which eventually changed the philosophy of the sport. Player prompted a simple but profound alteration of values. In essence, he made it quite clear he was not afraid to be seen actually trying to win. That, after all, was the only reason he prepared and trained so hard.

Not for him, the old-fashioned, game's-the-thing gentleness in which taking part was the only honourable objective. He wanted to win at all costs. He was not ashamed to show it and, while such naked ambition initially surprised the royal and ancient world, it was to become the pattern for others.

In a sense, the Player approach can be said to have played a pivotal part in creating a competitive climate which directly caused the astounding improvements in the standards of play as players of healthy aspirations realized the value of the Player Principle that Hard Work + Dedication = Success. Or, as he put it more earthly: 'The more I practise, the luckier I get.'

From the moment he took his place among the champions by winning the 1959 Open at Muirfield, Player was to be a relentless force upon the game and an influence far greater than the three British titles, one US Open, three Masters and two USPGA Championships attributed to him in the record books.

In many ways, he also brought a spiritual dimension to the game. Or rather, he examined the importance of a correct mental attitude and its influence on success. In so doing, he was ridding the game unwittingly of its old perceptions because, at its best, golf is a complete examination of a man — his skills and his character — and Player's own career was to be devoted to the development of both.

In all of this, he was a victim of circumstance. Indeed, his whole life can be seen as a saga of struggle and triumph against the odds. By the time he was nine, his mother had died and there began a solitary existence punctuated by occasional family traumas that served to teach this undersized young boy that in this world he could really only rely on himself.

More than this, those early shocks — the bereavement and a teenage accident in which he broke his back and was bedridden for almost nine months — taught him another enduring principle of life and golf: Play it as it lies — accept what's dealt and make the best of it. Simply forget about what might have been, and continue on.

Curiously, there seemed also to be a deeper missionary motive running parallel to Player's chosen career. He was, after all, a firm believer and made no secret of the Almighty's involvement in his success as though some solemn bargain had been struck between them. It was a zealous approach that his contemporaries at times found overpowering.

When he won his last Masters in 1978 with a staggering last-round 65 to catch all his young rivals napping, he revealed afterwards that he had constantly repeated a prayer throughout the round. Much earlier in his career, he recalled seeing

Player refused to abandon South Africa.

the 'vision' of his name on the 1965 US Open scoreboard long before he triumphed to complete his personal set of four Grand Slam titles.

The public perceived him as a fierce fighter on the golf course, determined to prevail by every justifiable means at his disposal. He likened himself to a boxer climbing into the ring. Consequently, the disparity between what he said and what he did often laid him open to charges of double standards.

He saw no such inconsistency. In any case, he was accustomed to both controversy and criticism. He held a wider significance in the world as one of South Africa's most famous globe-trotting figures. Against the background of apartheid problems in his own country he was made accountable — the apologist — wherever he went.

More than this, there were times when he was subjected to the most intense pressures and, as well, the intolerable burden of trying to play his best golf while being the target for political activists.

His life was threatened in the United States. Police cars patrolled the streets at night where he stayed. In the 1969 USPGA at Dayton, Ohio, demonstrators threw missiles at him and he was obliged to play the last round under police escort. Similar treatment awaited him in Australia and in France where he was also the target for anti-apartheid militants.

He could have slipped away from it in the manner of other sportsmen by leaving the country of his birth to set up home elsewhere, thereby offering the world both a disclaimer and condemnation of the regime. But, he refused and, by staying within his beloved South Africa, played more than a peripheral role in its painful but inevitable transformation.

On a purely personal and more tangible level, he has made immense contributions to this change. Next door to his home in Johannesburg, he built a magnificent multi-racial school for local children and set up a trust fund to help the young on a wider scale because he believed that the future of South Africa lies with the education of all its children.

The curious strand running through nearly all his greatest triumphs on the fairways is that each of them had a moment of crisis in which only the perfect match-winning stroke could save him. Indeed, his championship career began with drama and tears when he thought he had thrown the 1959 title away and had to wait all afternoon at Muirfield before he could be sure nobody would catch him.

His first Masters win involved an extraordinary mishap to Arnold Palmer, who needed only par on the last hole for victory and faced a comfortable approach shot from the middle of the fairway to become champion again. Arnie unaccountably bunkered his shot, thinned the recovery to the back of the green to take 6 and allow Player, watching the drama on television in the clubhouse, to take the green jacket.

His 1968 Open win at Carnoustie contained one of the greatest strokes of his career when, with Jack Nicklaus closing in, he thrashed a three wood over the Spectacles — the bunkers on the left of the 14th fairway — to a green he could not see to set up an eagle 3 which sealed that title for him.

At Oakland Hills in 1972, his USPGA victory will always be remembered for the blind shot he played over trees and a lake guarding the 15th green to secure a birdie chance on the final day and thwart the opposition.

And his momentous victory in the 1965 World Match Play Championship at Wentworth, when he was five down with nine holes to play against Tony Lema yet revived to defeat him, offered as much testimony to his indomitable spirit as it did to his tireless skill and stamina.

It would be wrong, however, to suggest that Player was the first champion to discover the true importance of commitment in golf. The other great heroes must all have possessed this necessary ingredient in some measure in order to succeed.

But the difference was that Player personified it. He gave it definition and dimension so that others could copy and follow in whatever measure they chose. He built up his physique through a punishing daily exercise routine and invariably took his weight-training equipment as excess baggage wherever he travelled in the world. To this day, when there seems no obvious urgency, he still pursues his daily routine.

He always believed in the value of a sound diet, though at times seemed to take the practice to eccentric lengths — the bananas, the raisins, the peanuts and the African mealie-mealie dishes — all, no doubt, of immense nutritional value at the time but more important because they revealed the lengths to which he would go to succeed.

There is, however, another aspect to this astounding life of Gary Player. His championship career spanned 19 years, second only to Jack Nicklaus, who endured for 24 years. Such longevity will never be witnessed again. The modern champions are shorter-lived. One question, therefore, may at first perplex students of the Player phenomenon.

It is not the obvious one of precisely how Player lasted for so long at the pinnacle of the game. But, rather, why it mattered so much for him to do so for all that time — particularly with all the sacrifice both personal and professional involved. The secret can be traced to Player's own guiding philosophy.

A talent unfulfilled is the greatest waste of all. The duty is to be the best. That too is probably the most important legacy that Player leaves for future generations — an unshirkable obligation to pursue talent to its limit whatever the cost.

On the fairways for five decades, Player personified the commitment necessary to be a lasting champion.

Joint leader Steve Pate wasn't pleased with his swing, but 'I putted very well.'

DAY

1

PATE, FLOYD START WITH 64s

BY ROBERT SOMMERS

Like all seaside courses, Muirfield, that wonderful layout beside the Firth of Forth, on Scotland's East Lothian coast, relies on wind to hold scoring in check. As the week of the 121st Open Championship approached, it seemed likely the 156-man field would be given all the wind they would want.

Throughout the weekend before the championship was to begin, gales ripped in from the west, turning Muirfield into as difficult an examination in golf as the most zealous guardian of par could dream of. Blend the wind with Muirfield's fast-running fairways, hardened by an eight-week drought, and scores seemed likely to reach unusually high numbers.

No one should rely on the weather. Like Pebble Beach in the early rounds of the US Open a month earlier, the wind didn't blow at Muirfield in the first round — at least not enough to speak of. What little wind came in blew light and soft and had no effect on shot or club selection. Barely a ripple disturbed the smooth surface of the Forth, and the upper branches of the trees

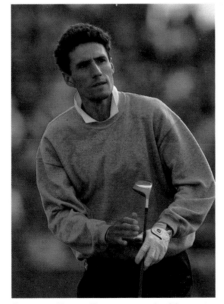

Amateur Daren Lee was out in 32.

in Archerfield Woods, flanking the eighth fairway, barely wavered in the breeze.

Although the conditions were benign, Muirfield did not exactly lay helpless, since on the softest days it remains among the more severe examinations of the game. But it was inviting.

Mark Calcavecchia gave the first indication that Muirfield could be ravaged. Off in the fourth group, at 7.45, Calcavecchia, the 1989 champion, reeled off four consecutive 3s, three of them for birdies. In the

mild weather his irons floated on unwavering flight toward the flagsticks, leaving him putts of 20 feet, 10 feet and five feet. He couldn't keep up this hot pace, though. Bogeys on the sixth and eighth, two strikingly difficult par 4s, brought him back to reality, but even so he played the first nine in 34, came back in 35, and shot 69.

Where Muirfield normally rejects the attempts of all but the most skilled golfers, the scoreboards were showing unfamiliar names throughout the day — Lee Janzen, Costantino Rocca, Jeff Maggert, Orrin Vincent, Larry Rinker, Daren Lee — all of them under 70 on a course a great many close to golf believe is the game's best.

On this day, though, Muirfield was pillaged. At the end of the long day (the first group left the first tee at 7.15 in the morning, and the last at 4.20 in the afternoon), 35 men had shot in the 60s, and another 21 had shot 70. Muirfield has a par of 36-35— 71.

Raymond Floyd, a relic of an earlier time, shot 64 and shared the first-round lead with Steve Pate, another American, who was born in 1961, the year Floyd became a professional. They stood a stroke ahead of Ian Woosnam, who was no surprise, and Gordon Brand, Jr., who was, with Nick Faldo another stroke back, tied with John Cook, twice a winner earlier on the American Tour, Janzen, an obscure young American who had played the minor Ben Hogan Tour in 1991, and Ernie Els, a young and strong South African.

Ripples of approval had followed Woosnam and

Paul Way (above, left) led off the 121st Open Championship at 7.15. Play ended nearly 14 hours later.

Raymond Floyd hit 17 greens in pursuit of the only major title he has never won.

Gordon Brand, Jr., (65) was within view of his birthplace.

Lee Janzen (66) followed veteran caddie Dave Musgrove.

John Cook (66) had two American victories.

After a bogey at No. 1, Andrew Magee came back with 67.

Faldo around Muirfield, but to find Floyd at the head of such a strong gathering of golfers amazed the galleries. He has been among the more durable golfers the game has known and, even as he stands on the brink of turning 50, he continues as a threat in every competition he enters.

Only a few men had played at this level at this age. Harry Vardon came within a stroke of tying Ted Ray for the 1920 US Open after he had turned 50; Ben Hogan hit 34 of 36 greens on the last day of the 1960 US Open within two months of his 48th birthday; and Jack Nicklaus won the 1986 Masters at 46. Floyd's longevity might outdo all of theirs.

Wonderfully supple and limber, Floyd keeps himself fit through exercises, principally drills that stretch the muscles. Through these workouts, he believes he has kept his backswing as fluid and as long as it has ever been, and he has been playing superb golf.

'I'm playing better golf now than I ever have,' he said. No one who watched him could argue. Granted Muirfield seemed as forgiving as it has ever been for an Open, Floyd's golf was of another world. He hit 17 of the 18 greens, missing only the 14th, a difficult par 4 of 449 yards playing into the prevailing westerly wind, and reaching the fifth, one of Muirfield's three par-5 holes, with his second shot.

Floyd bogeyed only the eighth, where his four-iron approach left him 35 feet from the hole, and he three-putted. Generally, though, he played superb irons that usually left him within holing distance. Of his eight birdies, he holed only one longer than 15 feet, a 30-footer that dropped for a 3 at the 12th, and he nearly holed his wedge to the third, leaving his ball only six or eight inches from the cup.

Even with his bogey, Floyd went out in 32, making five of his eight birdies on the first nine, beginning at

Ian Woosnam was aiming for 63 before his par, bogey finish left him with 65.

Nick Faldo (66) was aggressive in the calm conditions.

Ernie Els (66) had four South African victories.

the first, where he dropped a five iron within 12 feet. After his near eagle on the third, Raymond drilled a driver from the high fifth tee, then ripped a two iron onto the green. Even though the fifth played downwind all week, what breeze there was seemed quite light at the time, and so covering the 559 yards called for two first-class shots.

Raymond added three more birdies on the home nine, playing a lovely sand wedge inside six feet at the 11th, and then turning back into the wind and punching a six iron that drifted 30 feet away on the 12th. Coming to a stretch of holes that stand among Muirfield's most severe, he moved past the 13th, 14th and 15th in good order, although he had a scare on the 14th. His two-iron second drifted into a greenside bunker and nestled close to the steep front wall. Floyd played a stunning recovery within 10 feet, then ran the putt home.

Another par at the 16th, where he saved his 3 with a six-footer, brought him to the 17th, another long par 5 of 550 yards that once again played downwind. After another fine drive, Floyd ran his three iron over the green, chipped back, and made his final birdie of the day. Back in 32, he had his 64.

Reflecting on the day, Floyd said, 'To go out and hit 17 greens and to be on a par 5 in two and have chances to be on two others is about the best I can play. I don't expect to play better than that.'

Floyd had begun his round at 12.40. By the time he finished, Pate had already turned in his 64, the same score as Floyd's, but not the same kind of round. Although both of them had hit 17 greens, for the most part Floyd had hit his ball closer to the flagsticks than Pate. Where Raymond had played his approaches to the first three holes to 12 feet, 14 feet and eight inches, Pate faced two putts of 30 feet and another of 40. He made none of them, but he reached the green of the fifth with a drive and three iron 60 feet from the hole and managed to get down in two for his first birdie. Another followed at the sixth, where he holed from five feet, and still another when a six-footer dropped at the ninth.

Out in 33, Pate missed his only green at the 10th, but a sand wedge to three feet saved his par, and he played through the next two holes with no trouble. Still three under with six holes to play, Pate reeled off birdies on each of the next three holes, dropping him to six under, then added another at the 17th, where

Italy's Costantino Rocca (67) was playing well again.

Rocco Mediate (67) joined the American challenge.

he holed from 15 feet after reaching the green with two three woods and a sand wedge. Needing a par 4 at the 18th for 64, Pate drilled a two iron within 10 feet, setting up a possible 63, but he missed the putt. He had come back in 31.

With 65, Woosnam had never scored so low in a major competition, and even had a chance for a better score, but lost it at the 17th, the par 5 that was so reachable downwind, and 18th, at 448 yards one of the game's premier finishing holes. With 63 practically in hand, he failed to birdie the 17th, and then bogeyed the 18th, falling into a tie with Brand.

Woosnam had been grouped with Nicklaus, who had won the first of his Open Championships at Muirfield 26 years earlier, in 1966, and before he had teed off he worked with Bob Torrance, his coach, on the proper use of his legs. The session with Torrance seemed to help. Woosnam claimed his swing, an uncomplicated movement that can't go very wrong, never felt better.

Starting with a birdie at the second, at 351 yards Muirfield's shortest par 4, Woosnam added another at the fifth, then nearly threw it away when he pulled his tee shot to the seventh into a bunker. Climbing

Per-Ulrik Johansson (67) needed a 10-man play-off to qualify.

down into the pit, Woosnam disappeared from sight, but a flurry of sand, and his ball popped out, eased down the slope, and rolled 18 inches from the cup.

Thinking of the shot later, Woosnam confessed, 'That was one of the hardest shots I've ever had to play. I could have had a hundred goes at it and not got it as close as that.'

It was, indeed, a great boost, and seemed to buoy Woosnam's spirits. Birdies on the eighth and ninth and Woosnam was out in 32, four under par. Another birdie at the 10th, then two more at the 14th and 15th and he stood seven under with the 17th still to come. The 63 seemed certain. It fell apart when he tried to put too much into his drive, pulled it into the rough, then, strong as he is, couldn't tear through the grass with enough power to reach the green with his three iron. A pitch to 25 feet and two putts for his 5, then a drive into a bunker at the 18th assured a bogey finish.

Woosnam believed a 15-minute wait on the 17th tee caused him to lose concentration, and when he stepped up to his ball, he wasn't focused. He had planned to play a big drive and go for the eagle 3, but with the delay, his swing went haywire.

Unlike Woosnam, Brand isn't often found among the leaders on these big occasions, but he was at the peak of his game here. Perhaps the reason went beyond the work he had put in during the weeks leading up to the championship, directed by his father, a club professional. Then again, perhaps there were other reasons.

From the high ground, Brand could look across the Firth of Forth to Burntisland, where he was born. Perhaps the sight of home gave him inspiration, for he had broken 70 in the first round of the Open only once before, when he shot 69 at Sandwich seven years earlier.

Even though he was playing first-class golf, he felt slightly uncomfortable with his driver through most of the round, but he managed to fight through, setting off with three birdies on the first five holes, then adding another at the eighth.

With 32 on the first nine, Brand stood four under par, and since he had started a little after 2 o'clock, Pate had finished, and he knew he had to pick up three more strokes to catch him. A five-footer fell at the 10th. Two more to go, but the putts wouldn't fall. He nearly lost a stroke when he bunkered his drive on the demanding 14th, but he pitched safely out, then played a wonderful seven iron to nine feet and holed the putt for his par. He picked up his sixth birdie at the 17th, where he reached the green with a three iron, played the home nine in 33, and shot 65.

Lying two strokes behind the leaders, with his 66, Faldo seemed happy to be that close, particularly after his start. With the whole fairway open except for a bunker on the left, Faldo drove into the sand and found his ball in such an awkward position he had to stand with one foot in the sand and the other on the bunker face. With no shot to the green, he bogeyed.

He made up for that mistake on the fifth, where his two-iron second went over the green, and he chipped in from 25 yards for an eagle 3. Three quick birdies beginning at the eighth, and another at the 13th and he had played the nine holes beginning at the fifth in six under par. He stood five under par then and might reasonably have expected to reach six under with the 17th still to be played. It wasn't to be, though, and might even have been worse.

Nick pushed his second shot into the bunker carved into the side of a high mound that had to be carried to reach the green. Above all, though, he had to clear the hill, and when he did, his ball ran well past the cup. He parred.

Still five under and facing the tough home hole, Faldo played a loose drive that didn't go very far, then left his approach short of the green. He had to hole a nervous five-footer for his 4.

While his 66 fell a stroke short of his opening 65 at St Andrews two years earlier, he had played well enough to stand within reach of the lead.

'On a day like this,' Faldo said, 'you have to play aggressive golf. I was trying to hit the ball at the pins all the way, not to the percentage areas, because today we have a free run at it.'

Not everyone took advantage of the benign conditions, though. Ian Baker-Finch, the 1991 champion, who had ripped Royal Birkdale apart in the last round a year ago, shot 71; Davis Love III, one of the early sensations on the American Tour, never seemed to get the hang of links golf and shot 73, along with Tom Watson, who seems to have lost his flair for it. Curtis Strange, who can't hole a putt, shot 74; and Nicklaus, whose every Open might be his last, shot 75. Colin Montgomerie, the young Scot with so much promise, shot 76, lamenting, 'I reserved my worst round of the year for today.'

Several others were still in it, but they would need a stronger second round to close ranks. Tom Kite, whose game struggle with the weather and a severe course won the US Open for him in June, shot 70, along with Bernhard Langer, Fred Couples, the Masters champion, Payne Stewart, Jose Maria Olazabal and Paul Azinger, whose loose play on Muirfield's last two holes five years earlier had cost him the 1987 Open.

As usual, drawing a sizeable portion of the day's big gallery while he struggled with an attack of hay fever, Ballesteros sneezed his way around Muirfield and had to birdie three of the last seven holes to score his own 70.

In the excitement of the day, Paul McGinley's hole-in-one on the seventh was largely ignored; and hardly anyone gave much thought to the eagle John Cook scored on the 17th, which dropped him to 66, the same score as Faldo. It would become significant, as would the 17th hole.

Craig Parry (67) was hoping his 'experience at Augusta and Pebble Beach this year will help me.'

Directional signs and huge stands accommodated the mass of spectators, while a lucky few were secluded in Greywalls.

FIRST ROUND RESULTS

HOLE	1	2	3	4	5	6	7	8	9	10	11	12	13	14	15	16	17	18	
PAR	4	4	4	3	5	4	3	4	5	4	4	4	3	4	4	3	5	4	TOTAL
Steve Pate	4	4	4	3	4	3	3	4	4	4	4	4	2	3	3	3	4	4	64
Raymond Floyd	3	4	3	3	4	4	2	5	4	4	3	3	3	4	4	3	4	4	64
Ian Woosnam	4	3	4	3	4	4	3	3	4	3	4	4	3	3	3	3	5	5	65
Gordon Brand, Jr.	4	3	4	2	4	4	3	3	5	3	4	4	3	4	4	3	4	4	65
Lee Janzen	4	4	3	2	4	4	3	4	5	3	4	4	3	4	4	3	4	4	66
Nick Faldo	5	4	4	3	3	4	3	3	4	3	4	4	2	4	4	3	5	4	66
Ernie Els	4	4	4	3	4	4	3	3	5	4	3	5	2	4	4	3	4	3	66
John Cook	3	4	3	3	4	4	3	4	4	5	4	4	3	4	4	3	3	4	66
Costantino Rocca	4	4	4	3	4	3	3	4	5	4	4	4	2	4	4	3	4	4	67
Andrew Magee	5	4	4	2	4	4	3	4	5	4	4	4	2	4	3	3	4	4	67
Craig Parry	4	4	3	4	4	4	3	4	4	4	4	4	3	4	4	2	4	4	67
Per-Ulrik Johansson	4	4	4	4	5	3	3	3	4	4	4	4	3	3	4	3	4	4	67
Orrin Vincent	4	3	3	3	4	4	3	3	5	4	4	3	3	5	4	3	5	4	67
Rocco Mediate	4	4	3	3	4	4	4	4	4	4	3	4	3	4	4	3	4	4	67

HOLE SUMMARY

HOLE	PAR	EAGLES	BIRDIES	PARS	BOGEYS	HIGHER	RANK	AVERAGE
1	4	0	8	93	54	1	2	4.31
2	4	0	25	115	16	0	13	3.94
3	4	0	30	123	3	0	15	3.83
4	3	0	20	108	25	3	11	3.07
5	5	6	81	56	13	0	18	4.49
6	4	0	17	96	41	2	5	4.19
7	3	1	11	107	34	3	4	3.17
8	4	0	18	96	38	4	6	4.18
9	5	4	49	89	9	5	16	4.76
OUT	36	11	259	883	233	18		35.94
10	4	0	20	94	39	3	8	4.16
11	4	0	23	113	19	1	12	3.99
12	4	0	9	113	32	2	7	4.17
13	3	0	23	121	12	0	14	2.93
14	4	0	12	78	59	7	1	4.40
15	4	0	16	104	35	1	10	4.13
16	3	0	16	110	29	1	9	3.10
17	5	3	79	67	6	1	17	4.51
18	4	0	8	97	46	5	2	4.31
IN	35	3	206	897	277	21		35.70
TOTAL	71	14	465	1780	510	39		71.64

Players Below Par	56
Players At Par	24
Players Above Par	76

LOW SCORES

Low First Nine	Gordon Brand, Jr.	32
	John Cook	32
	Raymond Floyd	32
	* Daren Lee	32
	Orrin Vincent	32
	Ian Woosnam	32
Low Second Nine	Steve Pate	31
Low Round	Raymond Floyd	64
	Steve Pate	64

Raymond Floyd had already won this year in America, just months before joining the Senior Tour.

AT AGE 49, FLOYD DRIVES ON

BY MICHAEL WILLIAMS

If you put a helmet on his head, a grid in front of his face and dressed him in knickerbockers, Raymond Floyd would fit the part for the Super Bowl. He has the same high, wide shoulders of the American footballer, his body then tapering down to still relatively slim hips. His legs are long but his stride short, his step almost mincing.

Now approaching his 50th birthday, Floyd has been around in golf a long time, since 1963 in fact, which is only 12 months after Jack Nicklaus also turned professional. In that time he has not changed much. Nor has his game, which is arguably underrated.

In 1989 he came to Britain as the non-playing captain of the American Ryder Cup team which tied with Europe at The Belfry. Such status indicated that his career was, if not over, certainly coming to a conclusion. It was not. Two years later he was back in the team as a player, good enough indeed to go out top against Nick Faldo in the singles on the last day. He lost, but the two points he had earlier picked up in the foursomes and fourballs, each time with Fred Couples, to whom he has become a sort of father figure, were of particular value in the narrowest of American victories.

Floyd has always been the sort of man you would like at your side in a tight corner. There is, when he wants, a forbidding look about his eyes that posts a warning to anyone unwise enough to start looking for trouble. He is not, and never has been, a man to mess with. He is tough.

In March 1992 he got a telephone call in the middle of the night to tell him that his home at

Wife Maria has influenced Floyd's career.

Indian Creek, near Miami, Florida, had largely been burned to the ground.

Yet within a week he was back on Tour and won the Doral Open. It equalled Sam Snead's record of winning a tournament in four different decades and it made Floyd the oldest since Art Wall, who, at the age of 51, took the Milwaukee tournament in 1975.

And now, here at Muirfield in Floyd's 18th Open Championship since his first appearance at Royal Lytham in 1969, he raised another possibility. A first round of 64, which tied the lead with another American, Steve Pate, put him within sight, if not as it transpired also sound, of becoming the oldest winner of all; ahead even of Old Tom Morris, who was 46 years and 99 days when he took the title at Prestwick in 1867.

Even more appealing was the fact that Floyd now had the chance of becoming only the fifth player in history to complete the set of the four majors: the Open championships of Britain and America, the United States PGA and Masters. Gene Sarazen, Ben Hogan, Nicklaus and Gary Player are alone in conquering this quadrilateral of golfing peaks.

Floyd had won the USPGA twice, in 1969 and 1982, the Masters in 1976 and the US Open in 1986, the oldest winner at the time although he was subsequently overtaken by Hale Irwin. Only the Open Championship had escaped his clutches, although there were several occasions when he had been close or relatively close.

In 1976 at Royal Birkdale he was fourth, seven

strokes behind Johnny Miller; in 1978 he was in a group of four who tied for second, two strokes behind Nicklaus at St Andrews, and in 1981 he was tied for third, seven shots behind Bill Rogers at Royal St George's. Otherwise his record was unexceptional for a player who has become more exceptional the longer he goes on.

There is, it would seem, little doubt that the success of the American Senior Tour has made a lot of difference to what Lee Trevino once memorably called the 'round bellies.' It has provided golfers with an incentive to keep their games in shape so that when they reach the age of 50 they are ready and sharp for a second golfing life.

Once there was a time when even 35, or certainly 40, was regarded as the evening of a career. Tony Jacklin was one victim of such a belief, and it is very difficult to get the game back again once it has been allowed to drift. Floyd has never done that.

Certainly there was a time in the 1980s when his game did show serious signs of decline — 86th, 69th and 145th in the money list — and for a time he worked very hard on the technicalities of the swing. But it bored him and in the end he reverted to just letting the club swing naturally.

'I am so comfortable with what I am doing,' he remarked, 'that I can now leave the clubs alone for a while and then take them out and the swing is right there again. In the past, if I had taken two weeks off I might have come back and shot 80s for a month.'

The real clue to Floyd being a Peter Pan of golf, however, is more likely to be found in that he just enjoys competing. His swing has never been one of poetry and grace, for he rocks and lurches as his club describes more than one arc. It nevertheless repeats.

There is something of the hustler about him. In his bachelor days, Miami Beach and the Playboy Club in Chicago were among his more regular haunts. He had a connection with a topless female band and once he was approached by a then inexperienced British broadcaster who hesitantly suggested he was associated with the Mafia. Fixing him with that cold, steely look he can produce at will, Floyd replied that he had 'had some daft questions put to him in his time but ...' and the confused broadcaster, on whom as a practical joke the question had been planted, switched instantly to the merits of the third hole of the course where the interview was taking place!

Floyd is known as one of golf's greatest competitors.

Floyd was 32 when he married, and his wife, Maria, who has borne him three children, shaped the remainder of his career. Her influence has been considerable, never more so than when their house was largely burned to the ground. Floyd was woken in the early hours in San Diego, where he was preparing for the Buick Invitational.

'This was the worst thing that I could imagine ever happening to my family other than death,' he reflected later. 'We have basically lost everything we had — mementos and pictures and baby pictures and wedding things — we've lost it all.' It was of only partial consolation that the fire stopped short of his trophy room.

It was Maria who took control. 'There is not much you can do here,' she told him as they surveyed the ashes. 'Go back and play golf.' He did and won at Doral. It was the 22nd victory of his career, a prime example of instant mind over the sort of matter that would have reduced others to pulp.

Now that the turmoil and the shock of all that he has lost have been absorbed, Floyd's start to the Open Championship on the sort of benign day that broke down all of Muirfield's defences, so much so that more than a third of the field beat par, promised the biggest fairytale of all.

It was a model round of golf, Floyd's best by five strokes in an Open. What he found particularly satisfying was that he missed only one green, the 14th, in the correct number of shots. A two-iron second was badly plugged in the wall of a bunker but he played a magnificent explosion shot to 10 feet and holed the putt.

He did, however, drop one shot, taking three putts at the eighth for a 5. Otherwise it was all 3s and 4s, eight of them birdies. At the long fifth he was on in two with a drive and two iron. It cancelled out, he felt, the green he had missed at the 14th.

'I really do not think I have lost any length at all,' he said afterwards. 'I think the reason for that is my suppleness and flexibility. I still rotate my shoulders and keep my hips out of the way. I don't think the number you put on your age is the indicator. I feel pretty good, feel healthy and that is why I am playing well. There is no magic potion for that. All I do is a few stretching exercises each day but I do know that I am playing better golf this year than I have ever played.'

For someone who, when he won the Masters in 1976 at the same time equalled Nicklaus's record of 271, that was saying something. That was Floyd's greatest hour, or rather four days. Two opening 66s distanced him from the field. Two 70s followed and he won in a canter, by eight strokes.

Yet Augusta was also the scene of his greatest disappointment, the year 1990 when Faldo won for the second time. Everyone will remember that, the play-off, the tied first extra hole and then the seven-iron second shot Floyd dumped into the water to the left of the 11th green. It was an awful way to lose a major but Floyd has no personal recrimination. 'It was nearly a heck of a shot,' he maintains. 'No, that was not where I lost it. I lost it at the 17th.'

His recollections are as clear as if it were yesterday and inwardly he still seethes. 'Nick was playing ahead of me, but I had a shot lead coming to 17. I hit a good drive and all I had to the green was a shot of 135 yards, a nine iron.

'A birdie there and I would have been two ahead, but instead of going for a birdie, I played defensively, trying to make sure of a 4. I pulled it and that was the worst thing I could have done. It left me with a desperately difficult approach putt and I three-putted. It was a mental error. Nothing more. Nothing less.'

Conversely, Floyd was proud of his 64 at Muirfield, only one outside the championship record. 'My goal for years has been to win the British Open,' he confirmed. 'Throughout my career my goals have been channelled towards the major championships. I have always felt that in the world of golf that this is *the* Open Championship. In the States we have our own Open and everyone in the States considers that is "the one," but this is the golf Open of the world. If I go through my career without it I would be able to handle that, but it would be a nice embellishment to my career if I could win it.'

It did not happen. Subsequent rounds of 71, 73 and 72 drifted Floyd back to a share of 12th place, eight strokes behind Faldo. But for 24 hours this most lasting of all the 'round bellies' had been on top of the world. He may be again some day, for his 'sell by' date is by no means yet up.

He may still become the first to win a major event while on the Senior Tour.

It would be an interesting bet.

Nick Faldo's 130 aggregate broke the record of 132 first set by Henry Cotton 58 years ago.

FALDO SETS 36-HOLE RECORD

BY ROBERT SOMMERS

If there is one decisive moment in every great occasion, the moment that will be remembered when tales are told of the 1992 Open Championship arrived at 5.15 on the afternoon of 17 July. It was then that Nick Faldo rolled in a birdie putt on Muirfield's 12th green and took over the lead from Steve Pate, who at the moment Faldo's ball fell, had three-putted the 13th and dropped behind.

That Pate should be overtaken was inevitable, for Faldo was playing golf at a level hard to believe. With his birdie on the 12th he had made his third 3 in four holes, and he would add four more 3s over the next four holes — seven 3s in eight holes. At the end of the day Faldo not only would match the 64s both Pate and Raymond Floyd had shot in the opening round, he would have 130 for the first 36 holes, two strokes under the record that had been set first by Henry Cotton, until now the best of the modern English golfers, at Sandwich in 1934, and matched by both Faldo and Greg Norman at St Andrews in 1990.

Faldo shot his 64 in more severe weather than Floyd and Pate the previous day; the strength of the wind had picked up considerably overnight. Flags that fluttered weakly in Thursday's light wind snapped in the fresh breeze once again blustering in from the west, changing the way the players

John Cook (133) said he was excited to contend.

approached their shots. Where they had played their irons with their normal trajectory in the first round, they were punching them lower in the second, keeping them out of the breeze. In the changed conditions, the players with the most inventive imaginations, who happened to have the skill as well, held the advantage.

Because of the draw, the day shaped up as two distinct divisions, one in the morning, and the other in the afternoon. The morning saw Floyd trying to build on his opening 64, while John Cook and Gordon Brand, Jr., attempted to close in on him. Faldo, Pate and Ian Woosnam would continue their struggle in the afternoon.

Meantime, those who had not done well in the first round would have to wait out the day to see if they would qualify for the final two rounds.

Floyd went off at 7.45. Playing almost as well from tee to green as he had done in the first round, he did very little with it. Where he had hit 17 greens in the first round, he hit 15 in the second, but his approaches left him farther from the hole, and the putts were much more difficult. Floyd believed the wind hurt his putting style. To accommodate his unusually long, 38-inch putter, Raymond normally takes a decidedly upright stance. When it blows, he spreads his

American Donnie Hammond (135) had to pre-qualify then shot 65 in the second round.

Tom Purtzer (137) was in his first Open since 1982.

Jose Maria Olazabal (137) said his confidence was high.

feet and hunches lower over the ball, a position he doesn't like.

Raymond began by running off nine consecutive pars, missing birdie opportunities from inside 15 feet on four holes. A bogey and a birdie on the home nine and Floyd came in with a par round of 71 and 135 for the 36 holes. It wasn't nearly good enough to hold his position.

It had been a frustrating round; Floyd had played sound golf, given nothing away, and yet he lost ground; for while scoring in general didn't reach the level of the opening round — only 46 men broke par against 56 in the first round — at the end of the day he found himself not only five strokes behind the leader, but trailing three others.

Cook passed him first. Starting an hour later, he found right away he would have to alter his method of striking. He had played a normal four iron into the first green in the opening round, but with a much stronger wind coming directly at him, he took a two iron instead and kept his ball low. The ball, though, scooted into a greenside bunker, but playing what he called later one of the best bunker shots of his life, he recovered to three feet and saved par.

This set the tone of his round. He drove well, missing a few fairways but never so badly he had to

sacrifice a stroke, and while he found himself in three other bunkers over the next 17 holes, none cost him a stroke. On the other hand, he had at least one spectacular moment.

Three more pars took him to the fifth. With the wind coming from behind once again, it could be reached more easily with the second shot in spite of its 559 yards. After a decent drive, Cook lashed a three wood into a greenside bunker, then lofted his ball into the cup for an eagle 3. It was a terrific stroke of luck, enough to convince a golfer anything is possible.

Two strokes under par for the day now, and seven under for 23 holes, Cook had caught Pate, who hadn't started, then passed him. A sand iron to six feet on the sixth, and then a six iron to 30 feet on the eighth. Both putts fell, and suddenly Cook stood nine under par. Another birdie on the 11th and he had dropped to 10 under.

Cook's smooth ride hit a bump at the 12th, a downhill par 4 of 381 yards playing into the wind. His drive slipped off into the right rough. A seven iron, hooded to create a low flight, curled left and rolled off the green into the second of two deep greenside bunkers. He bogeyed, then under-clubbed his tee shot to the 13th, an uphill par 3, difficult

Gordon Brand, Jr., (133) was driving well.

Larry Rinker (137) birdied two of the first three holes.

Craig Stadler (142) went out in 32 but shot 70.

regardless of its length of less than 160 yards. With the wind slightly behind him, Cook played a nine iron. The ball hit short, ran forward a few feet, then turned and rolled back down the hill. A second bogey.

Cook had fallen back to eight under par, one stroke ahead of Brand, playing three holes behind him, and Pate, who still hadn't started. Floyd was holding at six under, along with Tom Purtzer, seldom a contender in major competitions, and Sandy Lyle, who had played through the 13th.

After giving his supporters so much hope, Lyle then missed from four feet on the 14th, costing him a bogey and dropping him to five under, tying him with Faldo, who was waiting for his starting time.

Still eight under after the 14th, Cook couldn't break free, for Brand had caught him. Starting at six under par with his sparkling 65 of the first round, Brand had been shaky at first, making a good 5 at the first after catching two bunkers, and missing a birdie from four feet on the second, but he turned his game around. He birdied the fifth and 10th and climbed within a stroke of Cook. Then Brand caught him with another birdie at the 13th, playing a full nine iron to three feet.

He didn't stop there. Within a hole he moved

Matching rounds of 71, 68 allowed James Spence (left) and Mark O'Meara to qualify for the final 36 holes.

Both on 138, Sandy Lyle and Lanny Wadkins (right) react as their putts go in, stay out.

ahead, drilling a three iron to nine feet on the 14th and holing the putt for another birdie. Nine under now, with the 17th, another potential birdie hole, still ahead. As Brand's putt fell on the 14th, Cook stood on the 17th fairway waiting for Lyle to finish.

Three under in the opening round, Lyle had sped around the first nine in 32, but he had nothing left. A poor second to the 17th cost him a chance at a birdie, and with a bogey on the 18th he came back in 38, shot 70, and never figured again.

The 17th green clear, Cook played only a six iron for his second shot and left it 30 feet from the hole. His first putt grazed the lip of the cup, and he birdied. Now he and Brand were tied once again at nine under. Cook parred the 18th, added 67 to his opening 66, and led at 133.

Brand held steady, added 68 to his opening 65, and matched Cook at 133. The drama of the morning had ended; the more gripping action of the afternoon was about to begin.

Pate teed off at 2.05, playing just ahead of Faldo. Steve had begun at seven under par, two strokes behind Cook and Brand, but he had caught them with birdies on the third, a good par 4 playing downwind, and the seventh, a stiff par 3 into the wind. Another birdie at the eighth and Pate had moved ahead to 10 under.

Meantime, beginning his rush to the front, Faldo had birdied both the fifth and sixth, but he had bogeyed the seventh, his only blemish on an otherwise inspired round. Another mis-played iron to the eighth landed him in a bunker and a wedge no better than 20 feet to the hole looked as if it might cost him another stroke, but with his reconstituted putting stroke, Nick rolled the ball into the cup.

Six under then, he lay four strokes behind Pate.

Nick Faldo (130) charged to one eagle and six birdies, against a lone bogey.

Tom Kite (139) was enjoying his US Open laurels.

Suddenly, though, Faldo picked up momentum.

Muirfield's ninth, a par 5 that normally plays about 495 yards, has often been described as the best hole on the course. Its fairway serpentines first right, avoiding a pair of bunkers nestled in shaggy grass and probing in from the left, then left, running close to the low stone wall that defines out of bounds. It is a truly wonderful hole that demands not only the intelligent shot, but control of nerves as well.

Everything hinges on the drive; it must hold the narrow fairway, pinched in by bunkers on the left and bordered on the right by grass that can reach a man's chest. Anything other than a first-class drive leaves little chance to be anywhere near the green with the second. Then the second shot must avoid the out of bounds and yet, under the right conditions, be played with enough length to reach the green. Often it is more prudent to lay up and pitch to the green with the third shot. Faldo went for it.

He hit a fine drive and followed it with a three-wood played as well as the club can be played. The ball rocketed off, disappearing for an instant in the gray overcast, then running onto the green. Just beginning to be caught up in the significance of the moment, the gallery roared when Nick's ball rolled within four feet of the cup.

Faldo had missed a birdie putt of about that length in the last round of the 1987 Open, but he would not miss here; the ball dived into the cup. An eagle 3, and now Nick stood at eight under par, off on one of the game's great bursts of scoring.

Pate was within reach now, and Faldo went after him. A birdie 3 at the 10th dropped him to nine under, and a par 4 at the 11th held him in place.

Up ahead, Pate could make no headway. Unreliable irons had left him far too much work to do on the greens. He was making his pars, but he struggled for each of them. Meantime he was being given a lesson in links golf, if only he had the wit to realize it. Through a stroke of good luck he had been grouped with Lee Trevino, who had won the Open here at Muirfield 20 years earlier. Trevino is always a joy to watch. He manipulates the ball so well, keeping it low into the wind, letting it float on the carrying breeze, turning it right or left with the changing demands. Playing to the 12th, Lee punched a low iron that bore through the wind straight at the flag, hit a little short and bounded slightly right, within birdie range.

Pate's approach, played from the fairway, flew higher and settled on the left rear of the green, a long way from the hole. Two putts saved the par, but his loose irons caught up with him on the 13th. With the flagstick toward the front, Pate's tee shot rolled to the extreme back of the green, perhaps 60 feet from the cup. It was asking too much for him to salvage still another par from so great a distance. He bogeyed, dropping to nine under par.

Just as Pate stepped up to putt his ball, Faldo was playing to the 12th. After another first-class drive, Nick played a stunning low eight iron that knifed through the wind and settled 15 feet from the hole. The putt fell and he had another birdie 3, moved to 10 under par, and took over the lead.

Pate's troubles kept on. He missed the 14th green, taking a second consecutive bogey, fell to eight un-

Paul Azinger (139) was back, but not a contender.

Early-year star Tony Johnstone (143) barely qualified.

Bernhard Langer (142) was struggling with his game.

der, and walked to the 15th tee scratching his head and wearing a puzzled expression.

With Pate crumbling and Woosnam on his way to 73, Faldo took command.

Few men have played at such a high level. Trusting his swing and feeling comfortable with every club, he gave the impression he could make the ball do whatever he willed. A nine iron to 15 feet on the 13th, two putts and another 3. A drive and three iron to the 14th and still another. Then a drive and five iron to the 15th and a 15-footer fell for yet another. One more at the 16th, a par 3, and Faldo had scored his ninth 3 of the round. He had fallen to 12 under for 34 holes, seven under for the round, and needed two more pars for 64.

On the 17th he hit what he said was one of three poor shots he played, an uninspired five iron that lacked the zip to reach the green. An indifferent chip, and he made 5 rather than the 4 he might have expected.

Now he faced the menacing 18th, but it held no terror. Still bursting with confidence, he swung smoothly into his drive, then rifled a three iron 25 feet from the cup. Two putts, 64, and 130 for 36 holes.

Moments earlier Pate had stumbled home with 5s

on both the 17th and 18th, come home in 37 after an outgoing 33, shot 70, and dropped into fourth place, at 134, four strokes behind Faldo, one behind Cook and Brand. Floyd, in turn, lay a stroke behind Pate, along with the surprising Ernie Els and Donnie Hammond, who usually isn't found among this company in the big championships. Surprising everyone, Hammond streaked around Muirfield in 65, the second best score of the day. With Faldo playing as he had, though, no one seemed to notice.

Smiling, Faldo looked at his 130 and said, 'It'll be done, but good luck to someone trying to do 129.' Faldo was unusually expansive, declaring this to be the best round he had ever played in an Open. He said, 'I just felt so good inside, and I kept on hitting really good shots, so I thought, "Well, let's keep rolling on." Everything was so comfortable. No matter what club I had in my hand, it felt just right. I've never had that feeling over a whole round. When you consider where we are and what we're doing, that every shot is marked in history, it really is unique.'

The 36-hole cut fell cruelly at 143, one stroke over par, and caught some of the great players of this and past eras. The championship was the poorer for the loss of Jack Nicklaus, whose swing was not the assured movement we had come to know over the years, and Tom Watson, whose time is running out if he is to win his sixth Open. Both men had won at Muirfield in the past, Nicklaus in 1966 and Watson in 1980. Both men shot 148. Gary Player, another Muirfield winner, went out as well, with 146.

Sadly, Seve Ballesteros fell, too, stumbling to 75 in the second round and posting 145 for the two rounds. Fred Couples, who looked so unbeatable early in the year, played a loose 78 in the second round and fell out with 148. After a grim 76 in the opening round, Colin Montgomerie had little chance to make it; his 70 in the second wasn't nearly good enough, and he dropped out as well.

Others barely squeaked through. Ian Baker-Finch, the defender, slipped in at 142; Greg Norman made it with 143 as well, and John Daly, the game's newest siege gun, had to par the 18th to qualify for the last two rounds, and he did, one more spear-carrier in a cast so dominated by one man.

John Daly (143) shot 69 to make the 36-hole cut.

SECOND ROUND RESULTS

HOLE	1	2	3	4	5	6	7	8	9	10	11	12	13	14	15	16	17	18	
PAR	4	4	4	3	5	4	3	4	5	4	4	4	3	4	4	3	5	4	TOTAL
Nick Faldo	4	4	4	3	4	3	4	4	3	3	4	3	3	3	3	3	5	4	64-130
John Cook	4	4	4	3	3	3	3	3	5	4	3	5	4	4	4	3	4	4	67-133
Gordon Brand, Jr.	5	4	4	3	4	4	3	4	5	3	4	4	2	3	4	3	5	4	68-133
Steve Pate	4	4	3	3	5	4	2	4	5	4	4	4	4	5	3	3	5	5	70-134
Raymond Floyd	4	4	4	3	5	4	3	4	5	5	4	4	3	4	4	3	4	4	71-135
Donnie Hammond	4	4	3	2	5	5	2	3	4	4	4	3	3	5	4	3	3	4	65-135
Ernie Els	4	3	3	3	5	5	3	4	5	4	3	4	3	4	4	3	4	5	69-135
Tom Purtzer	4	4	4	3	4	4	3	4	4	4	3	4	3	5	3	4	4	5	69-137
Jose Maria Olazabal	5	4	3	3	4	4	3	4	4	3	3	5	2	4	4	3	5	4	67-137
Larry Rinker	4	3	3	3	5	4	3	4	5	5	4	4	2	4	4	3	4	4	68-137

HOLE SUMMARY

HOLE	PAR	EAGLES	BIRDIES	PARS	BOGEYS	HIGHER	RANK	AVERAGE
1	4	0	1	82	54	19	1	4.61
2	4	0	24	110	22	0	13	3.99
3	4	0	35	110	10	1	16	3.85
4	3	0	23	119	14	0	14	2.94
5	5	10	77	62	6	1	18	4.43
6	4	0	18	109	28	1	10	4.08
7	3	0	11	110	30	5	4	3.19
8	4	0	16	97	42	1	8	4.18
9	5	2	39	96	16	3	15	4.87
OUT	36	12	244	895	222	31		36.14
10	4	0	13	94	46	3	5	4.25
11	4	0	21	105	28	2	12	4.07
12	4	0	17	110	25	4	9	4.11
13	3	0	13	120	23	0	10	3.06
14	4	0	5	78	65	8	2	4.49
15	4	0	12	102	40	2	6	4.21
16	3	0	10	116	28	2	7	3.14
17	5	7	69	77	2	1	17	4.49
18	4	0	9	86	52	9	3	4.40
IN	35	7	169	888	309	31		36.22
TOTAL	71	19	413	1783	531	62		72.36

Players Below Par	46
Players At Par	24
Players Above Par	86

LOW SCORES

Low First Nine	Jose Coceres	32
	John Cook	32
	Donnie Hammond	32
	Robert Karlsson	32
	Sandy Lyle	32
	Malcolm Mackenzie	32
	Peter Senior	32
	Craig Stadler	32
Low Second Nine	Nick Faldo	31
Low Round	Nick Faldo	64

There was something for everyone at the Open — food, drink or a stroll in the Exhibition Tent.

The Masters champion, Fred Couples was expected to play well at Muirfield. He missed the cut by five strokes.

WHERE HAVE FAVOURITES GONE?

BY MARINO PARASCENZO

Golfers don't wear their hearts on their sleeves, they wear their games on their faces. Seve Ballesteros, for example. When things are going great, he's stone-faced. When they're not, he looks like an El Greco storm brewing. To go back a ways, Ben Hogan's expressions ranged from scowl to scowler. That's golfers, or at least some of them. No matter how good the last shot was, they know the next one will be worse.

Not Ben Crenshaw. Here's a man at peace. Or he's resigned to the notion that golf will be golf, so he can't hold his good nature in check for long. If he's not smiling, he's getting ready to smile. Which is why he could not be unpleasant to the bartender at Greywalls, the hotel next to Muirfield.

It was Sunday, the start of Open Championship week, the first day of qualifying. Crenshaw had to qualify this time. He finished his first round at North Berwick, then came back to Greywalls, and sauntered up to the bar with a hint of a smile.

'May I have,' Crenshaw said to the bartender, 'an arsenic, please.'

Crenshaw had a point there. By the end of the second round, he could have filled the hotel bar with a lot of big-name friends. When the 36-hole cut came on Friday, this Open Championship turned out to be unusually brutal for the rich and famous. Those who missed the cut would make a pretty strong field at any tournament.

You could start with the qualifying tournament. Now, it is not a certainty, but it's at least reasonable to believe that golfers the quality of Crenshaw, tested veteran and winner of the Western Open on the

Colin Montgomerie went out early.

American Tour just the previous week, and young American Phil Mickelson, were cinches to qualify. Not so.

The winds didn't help. The Open Championship would be more or less ruffled by winds, just enough to keep up appearances. But the real winds, those 40 mile-an-hour bursts that bend flags and break spirits, hit during the qualifying tournament. What had Crenshaw ordering an arsenic neat was the 79 he shot in the first round. He made a come-back for 71 on Monday, but that wasn't enough to save him. Mickelson, one of the most heralded amateurs since Jack Nicklaus, had an automatic berth in the Open as a Walker Cup player, but he lost the exemption when he turned professional, and had to try to qualify. He did not. He shot 80 in the first round. He rebounded for 68 in the second. He also was gone.

The Open hadn't even started yet. Things were going to get worse. By Friday night, such names as Ballesteros, Rodger Davis, Jeff Sluman, Colin Montgomerie, Tom Watson, Nicklaus, Gary Player, Fred Couples, Davis Love, Curtis Strange and brothers Naomichi and Masashi Ozaki were down the road.

The most prominent victim was Ballesteros. An Open without Ballesteros is like an Open without wind and rain. He had made that famed champion's march up the 18th fairway three times. The fourth was in the cards this time, and he sensed it. 'I'm very much a player who needs a little bit of inspiration,' Ballesteros said, 'and I'm waiting for that.' What he got instead was 70-75—145 and an early trip home. Ballesteros first entered the Open in 1975, when he was just 18 years old. He missed the cut that year. He made the cut the next 14 years, missed in 1990, made it in 1991, and now missed again — only three missed cuts in 18 Opens. When he made that march up the 18th fairway this time, he had tears in his eyes. But not from crying. It was hayfever. No alibis, though. 'It wasn't the hayfever,' Ballesteros said. 'I played terrible golf, and I didn't deserve anything better.'

Ballesteros was within a whisker of making the cut. All he needed was a par at No. 18. He missed the green, missed again, pitched on weakly, left a 40-foot putt 10 feet short and had to get that one down for a double-bogey 6. His 145 aggregate missed the cut by two strokes, both left at the 18th.

The Ozaki brothers never really had a chance, either. Naomichi, better known as Joe, started with 72, then two big crashes in the second round did him in. He double-bogeyed No. 7, triple-bogeyed No. 14 and shot 76—148. Brother Masashi, or Jumbo, a three-time winner on the 1992 Japan Tour, found the second nine tough to crack. He failed to get a birdie there in two days. He did, however, make seven bogeys — three the first day, well spaced-out, and four in the second round, all in succession, from No. 10. He finished with 74-86—150.

From the Close-But-No-Cigar Fraternity came Davis and Eduardo Romero. Davis was of special interest because he had almost won the 1987 Open at Muirfield. He never got close this time. After a level-par 71 start, he limped home with a double bogey at the 12th and bogeys at the 13th and 14th holes, for 74 and 145. Romero, the big-hitting Argentinian, stirred things up in the 1989 Open when he was mauling Royal Troon's par 5s for an eagle and three birdies in the first round. He stayed in the hunt until taking 75 in the third round. No such luck this time. He started with a four-birdie, four-bogey 71, then started and finished the second round with double bogeys for 77—148.

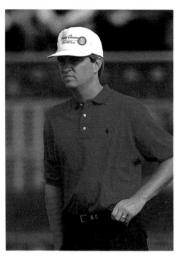

Davis Love III didn't look like a $1 million winner.

Two groups out of Charles Dickens came under the microscope — Opens Past and Opens Future.

The Opens Past were largely ceremonial. Watson, age 42, owns five Open titles, and Nicklaus, 52, three, and neither was playing well enough to expect another victory. Said Watson, 'I'm not thinking about winning a sixth Open, but I would like it.' Said Nicklaus, 'This may be my last Open. Then again, I may play in 10 more.' The shock came early for Nicklaus, a double bogey at the first hole on Thursday morning. He returned 75-73—148. Watson got crushed by No. 14, taking a double bogey each day. His rounds were 73 and 75. Maybe it was fitting that, if they had to miss the cut, they did it practically arm-in-arm, with matching 148 aggregates.

Now, the Opens Future:

Three comparatively new, comparatively young muscle-men are staking their place in the world of golf. They are Montgomerie, a Scot, and two Americans, Couples and Love. Couples had pretty much ruled American golf for months, and strengthened his grip with three victories, most notably the Masters in April. He was joined by Love, who also won three tournaments, and each had won over $1 million by the time of the Open Championship. Montgomerie was not enjoying that kind of success on the European Tour, but clearly he was in good company. By all indications, the three are among the heirs apparent in golf. But you couldn't tell from this week.

Montgomerie had almost won the US Open just a month earlier. It took a strong finish by Sluman, and then Tom Kite, the winner, to push him back to third place. And now he was at Muirfield trying to become the first home-born Scot in 82 years to win the Open. He had even changed his approach to the majors. He had cut back on his last-minute practice. It didn't help.

Caddie Allan and Curtis Strange finished on 147.

'What do you want me to say?' Montgomerie snapped at a journalist. 'Of course I'm disappointed. How would you feel about missing the cut in the Open?'

He gave himself too much of a load. He went seven over par in the space of 10 holes in the first round. The crippling blow was a double-bogey 5 at the 16th. He shot 76. He saw some light in the second round, when he played the first 12 holes in three under par, and got back to only two over par for the championship. Then another double bogey, at the 15th, finished him. He shot 70—146.

Couples had come in trying to understand Muirfield. 'I didn't play well here in 1987, so Muirfield is not one of my favourite courses,' he said. 'Hopefully I'll have a good week and like it more.' Couples, playing in the same group as Montgomerie, opened with 70, which included three birdies. Then came the plunge. He couldn't buy a birdie in the second round, and was struggling along on four bogeys until he reached the 18th hole. There, he crashed to a triple-bogey 7 for 78—148. He was asked about it. 'I've got a car waiting,' he said.

Muirfield gave Love no false hopes at all. The double bogey was his graveyard. He double-bogeyed the 18th the first day, and in the second round, he double-bogeyed No. 12, then the 18th again. His scorecard totalled 73-77—150.

Seve Ballesteros suffered from hayfever — and 'terrible' golf.

Sharing second place, John Cook (203) was impressed by the Open crowds. He said, 'I wish I could import them home.'

DAY

3

IT'S FALDO'S – TO WIN OR LOSE

BY ROBERT SOMMERS

The gallery began gathering at Muirfield early on the Saturday of the third round, clogging the narrow road that threads through the tiny village of Gullane, the only access to the golf course, planning to position themselves for a glimpse of Nick Faldo, whom most spectators were convinced held his third Open Championship in his hand. The next two rounds served only to determine who would come in second.

Bookmakers were even more confident. They had backed Faldo down to 4-7.

Quite a few years have passed since a golfer has stood so far above the field that we have expected him to win

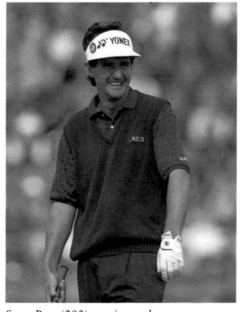

Steve Pate (203) was in a rules controversy.

whenever he put himself in position to win on the big occasions, especially when he had led halfway through the championship. Going back more than half a century, there was Bobby Jones, who was *expected* to win *every* time he played. Later Ben Hogan made a career of demolishing the competition, and then Jack Nicklaus became the favourite in his every appearance.

Perhaps Faldo hadn't reached that high a level, but it was obvious the day would revolve around how well he played, whether anyone would put pressure on him with a superb round of their own, and how well Nick would stand up to it. The great players have shown the strength of character to fight off assaults from their challengers.

Faldo would face a series of those challenges — from John Cook, who was paired with him in the

last grouping of the day, from Gordon Brand, Jr., Donnie Hammond, Ernie Els, and the most lasting from Steve Pate. All of them would fall short, and when darkness finally settled over the old links, Faldo ended the day gaining a stroke on the field, leading by four strokes rather than three.

That Faldo did not play up to his second round could be forgiven. Few men have reached that height under the intense emotion of the Open Championship. Asking him to repeat would have been asking far too much. Nevertheless, he returned his third consecutive score in the 60s, shooting 69 and finishing the 36 holes in 199, matching the record score he had set himself two years earlier at St Andrews.

Furthermore, in a round of wild swings of scoring when one player after another made a run at him, he savoured the immense satisfaction of throwing everyone off, of seeing all the challengers wilt under the tension. He alone held his composure and avoided grievous error, although he made the occasional mistake.

Nevertheless, during the long afternoon, in which Faldo and Cook started after 3 o'clock, he fought off every threat. Pate actually caught him, but then fell back with some shoddy golf; Cook closed in on him, but again couldn't keep up; and Brand, once only a stroke behind, collapsed over the closing holes.

We also saw a rules controversy settled, one that could have cost Pate another stroke for causing his

Ernie Els (205) was happy with his position.

ball to move before he played a chip onto the fifth green. The R and A ruled no penalty.

The weather seemed fairly unsettled through the day. Once again dark grey clouds hung overhead, but they broke occasionally, letting the bright warm sun break through, then closing in once more, spiting rain.

The wind blew out of the west still again with some force, rippling the tall grass with velocities from 20-25 miles an hour. Down to 75 men now, the field had played this wind every day, which might have accounted for the generally low scoring. They had learned to club themselves, and could attack the course with much more assurance than if the wind had shifted direction from day to day. Only the wind's relative strength could have caused them to hesitate over their selection of clubs and types of shots.

Off with Brand in the pairing ahead of Faldo and Cook, Pate started with a wild burst of scoring. After par figures on the first two holes, he birdied the next four in succession, only the fifth from long range. There he holed a putt from 30 feet after an incident that could have caused a penalty.

Pate's second shot, a five iron, settled on the upward slope of a greenside bunker, hanging in place by a few strands of grass. After a few practice swings, Pate set his feet and placed his clubhead behind the ball. Taking one more glance at the pin, he looked down at the ball, then stepped quickly away. Obviously dismayed, he summoned Andy McFee, a rules official with the European Tour, who was acting as referee.

Pate explained that although he did not see his ball in motion, he believed it had moved. The question then became whether or not Pate had grounded his club. He agreed he might have touched the ground a few inches away, but not directly behind the ball, which would have constituted addressing the ball, a key element in the rules of golf. Had the ball moved after address, which is defined as having taken your stance and grounded your club, Pate would have been penalized a stroke and would have been required to return it to its original position.

The officials on the spot took Pate's word that he

Seldom in trouble, Nick Faldo (199) played his bunker shots well, including one to three feet at No. 10.

Payne Stewart (214) was in his usual colourful attire.

Jose Maria Olazabal (206) thought he was too far behind.

Chip Beck (206) shot 67 with five birdies and one bogey.

Greg Norman (213) wasn't putting well.

Putting for eagle at No. 5, Cook had to settle for birdie. However, he got an eagle by pitching in at No. 9.

hadn't grounded his club, and therefore had not addressed the ball. Still lying 2, Pate chipped on, holed his third consecutive birdie, then hit a six iron within six feet and rolled in another on the sixth hole.

Pate stood 12 under par then, but Faldo had birdied the fourth, which had been giving up more birdies than any of the four par 3s. Measuring 180 yards, but playing downwind, it called for nothing more than a pitch. Faldo lofted a soft nine iron and holed from eight feet. With that putt he fell to 13 under par, then played extremely steady golf through the rest of the first nine. If they can be called blemishes, he failed to birdie either the fifth or the ninth, which he might have done with better putting.

He reached the fifth with his second shot, then three-putted from 45 feet, and he pushed his second shot to the ninth onto a mound to the left of the green, played an indifferent chip no closer than eight feet, then ran his putt four feet past. He regained his composure and holed it.

Pate, meantime, had fallen to 12 under par after his birdie on the sixth, and had closed to within one stroke of Faldo. With the ninth lying ahead, offering a reasonable opportunity for still another birdie, he was in position to shoot 31. Quickly, though, he dropped a stroke when his tee shot into the headwind fell short and rolled into the gathering bunker on the right of the seventh green. He played a weak recovery from an awkward stance and bogeyed, and then he butchered the ninth.

After driving into the high grass that lines the narrow, serpentined fairway, he tried to recover with nothing more ambitious than a nine iron. In grass that tall and dense, the club twisted in his hands, throwing the ball left into the rough on the other side. Playing still another lofted club from this tangled grass, he almost had the club torn from his hands. Still another shot from a horrid lie fell short. Instead of the anticipated birdie, he made 6. Still, he had turned in 34, picked up two strokes on par, and stood at 10 under, three behind Faldo.

More trouble lay ahead for Faldo. Brand had picked up ground on par as well by playing both par-5 holes on the first nine superbly. He reached the fifth green with a five iron and got down in two putts for his 4, and on the ninth ripped into a three iron that tore through the wind and rolled onto the green.

Long-shots Malcolm Mackenzie (left) and Sweden's Robert Karlsson (208) were both on line for top-10 finishes.

He missed an eagle by inches, and birdied again. Like Pate and Cook, he stood 10 under par.

Cook had saved himself from a mediocre round with one shot. He had started badly, driving into the bunker set on the left edge of the first fairway and had no shot to the green. He bogeyed, then saved par after a poor approach to the second had left him far from the hole. He regained the stroke he had lost on the first with a five iron of more than 200 yards into the fifth green, then watched his eagle putt, struck dead on line, stop only an inch or so short of the cup. Even par for the day, but still nine under for 41 holes, Cook three-putted the seventh when a shaky four iron left him 50 feet from the cup.

Now he stood eight under par, trailing Faldo by five strokes. A good drive and a better three wood and his ball lay about five yards short of the ninth green, perhaps 25 yards from the hole, in position to birdie with a good pitch-and-run.

Cook is dangerous from this distance. Early in the season he had chipped into the hole twice in the play-off of the Bob Hope Classic.

He settled over the ball, drew back his pitching club, then seemed to hit the ball too hard. It carried to the green, ran toward the pin with good speed, then rammed against the stick and dropped into the cup. An eagle 3, and now Cook had shaved par by one stroke on the first nine. At 10 under par, he had climbed back within three shots of Faldo.

In the heat of a struggle, Nick doesn't normally give strokes away, though. Anyone who could catch him would have to play outstanding golf. Nick had bogeyed only twice over 45 holes, on the first hole of the championship and again on the seventh in the second round.

Now, though, he bunkered his approach to the 10th. No matter; his recovery ran straight for the hole and looked as if it might drop for a birdie. It barely missed, then rolled three or four feet past. Except for a couple of instances, Faldo had been deadly from this distance. He had saved par on the first hole with a putt of a bit more distance, and again at the eighth, where he had pulled his approach. He had missed some as well, for example on the fifth, where he had one of his rare three-putt greens. Here on the 10th his putt slid past the cup. He had bogeyed, dropping back to 12 under.

At about this time Pate had played a wonderful approach to the 11th. From about 100 yards out, he had lofted a pitch that hit toward the front centre of this hard and fast green, took a gentle turn to the right, and rolled within a foot or so of the cup for a tap-in birdie. Back to 11 under par, just a stroke off the lead.

One hole later, he holed a long, breaking putt from off the 12th green. Now 12 under, he had caught Faldo.

Brand, meantime, was dropping out of the chase. Out in 34, which had dropped him to 11 under par for 45 holes, Brand stood just a stroke behind Faldo after Nick bogeyed the 10th. He could go no further. With the lead within reach if only he could make more birdies, Brand laboured through a series of agonies. He lost one stroke on the 12th, where he drove into the rough, and fell two strokes back. Worse was on the way.

Cook was holding steady at 10 under, and while Hammond had made up some ground, he wasn't within range just yet. Up ahead Ian Woosnam had made a move with two birdies on the first nine, but he needed something sensational to climb within reach of the lead. Instead of that electric moment, he double-bogeyed both the sixth and seventh. For the second time his tee shot on the seventh flew into a bunker, but there would be no miraculous recovery here. Fuming at his slightly buried lie, Woosnam

Ian Woosnam (208) complained of too much sand in the bunkers and poor putting.

played an indifferent shot that scooted off the far side of the green. A chip that could have been better and two putts cost him a 5. Further birdies on the 11th and 12th saved a 70 finish, but he fell from among the leaders and never reappeared.

Raymond Floyd, too, was having an indifferent day, shooting 73 and like Woosnam dropping from sight; and 67s from Chip Beck and Hale Irwin, the best rounds of the day, did nothing for them. The battle would remain among those at the top now.

Still playing only a hole behind, as he had through the first two rounds, Faldo watched Pate's progress. Again the 12th turned into a pivotal hole. Faldo had birdied the 12th on Friday just as Pate had bogeyed the 13th. On Saturday, though, Pate nearly birdied the 13th. His tee shot rolled off the back of the green, but his chip hung on the lip of the cup.

With 67, Hale Irwin tied for the day's low round.

Coming down the 12th at about this time, Faldo played a dangerous approach that settled within 15 feet or so of the hole, but on the left of the pin. Another yard or so left, and his ball could have tumbled into one of those deep greenside bunkers. No matter; Nick holed the putt for another birdie. He was back in the lead, and he would be tough to catch.

Now Pate played some shaky holes, dropping strokes on both the 14th and 15th, and Brand played even worse, driving into a bunker on the 14th and taking a double bogey without ever hitting a decent shot. Standing on the 15th tee, he snap-hooked another drive and suffered another bogey. He had lost four strokes in four holes.

Cook still held on at 10 under, tied with Pate, and Faldo was cruising along at 13 under.

Nick was playing copybook golf — an eight iron to the 13th, two putts from 25 feet; driver and a low two iron to the 14th, again two putts from 25 feet; driver and five iron to the 15th, still another 25-footer.

The gallery followed along in awe, cheering his every shot, then rushing for position up ahead, then standing silently as he set himself for the next. As he crouched over his putt on the 15th, an awesome stillness settled over the old links; not a sound could be heard except the distant barking of a dog. Then even the dog himself hushed as Nick set himself for the putt. It missed, but he had another par.

Up ahead, Pate steadied himself by birdieing the 17th, but he drove into a bunker on the 18th, costing him a stroke there; and he settled for a score of 69 for the day and 203 for the 54 holes, still 10 under par. In a strange sort of round, Pate had birdied seven holes and had bogeyed five. He had parred only six.

Brand had birdied the 17th as well, but he shot 72 and 205, leaving him eight under par.

Faldo had opened a five-stroke lead on Cook when John bogeyed the 14th after a poor approach with a three iron, but he matched Faldo's pars on the next two. They came to the 17th knowing one of them at least would birdie.

Faldo hit the longer drive, and so Cook would play

Team Lyle, Sandy and Yolande, were on 208.

Raymond Floyd (208) missed an eagle at No. 17 and shot 73.

his second shot first. His ball lay in the whispy rough about 225 yards from the green. Once again going with his three iron, he played a terrific shot that hit well short, bounded along the hard ground, and rolled well on, perhaps 30 feet left of the cup, tucked behind the high mound on the right.

From about 10 yards closer, Faldo hit a three iron as well, but his ball rolled over the green into the shortish grass in back. Nick chipped within three feet, about the same distance as the putt he had missed on the 10th, but he holed it here. Cook rolled his eagle putt within a foot of the cup. Both men birdied, Cook slipping to 10 under, the same as Pate, and Faldo now stood 14 under.

While Faldo once again played copybook golf to the 18th — drive and two iron to 20 feet — Cook struggled. Like Pate he drove into the fairway bunker and had no shot at the green. He pitched out perhaps 170 yards from the green, then played a wonderful iron about 10 or 12 feet left of the pin. Faldo holed out in two for his par, and Cook dropped his putt as

well. A par 4 and a round of 70 on a day when he was not at his best. He was in with 203, tied with Pate in second place.

As Faldo's last putt dropped, the gallery roared. Nick had shot 69, and had matched his own record of 199 for 54 holes. He bent over and picked his ball from the cup, then raised his right hand, acknowledging the cheers from the spectators. He wore an expression more of relief than of pleasure, and with tightly set lips, he strode off the green.

In three remarkable and memorable rounds over a stern and demanding course, for two days buffeted by moderately high winds, Nick had run off 13 birdies, two eagles, and had bogeyed only three holes. He had played overpowering golf, the kind we rarely see. He would go into the last round leading Pate and Cook by four strokes, with Els, the young South African, defying the odds as he held on at a stroke farther back, along with Brand and Hammond, all at 205. In reality, though, Faldo's only serious opposition lay within himself.

THIRD ROUND RESULTS

HOLE	1	2	3	4	5	6	7	8	9	10	11	12	13	14	15	16	17	18	
PAR	4	4	4	3	5	4	3	4	5	4	4	4	3	4	4	3	5	4	TOTAL
Nick Faldo	4	4	4	2	5	4	3	4	5	5	4	3	3	4	4	3	4	4	69-199
Steve Pate	4	4	3	2	4	3	4	4	6	4	3	3	3	5	5	3	4	5	69-203
John Cook	5	4	4	3	4	4	4	4	3	4	4	4	3	5	4	3	4	4	70-203
Ernie Els	4	4	4	4	4	4	3	4	5	4	4	4	3	4	4	3	4	4	70-205
Donnie Hammond	5	3	4	3	4	4	3	4	4	4	4	4	3	5	5	2	4	5	70-205
Gordon Brand, Jr.	4	4	4	3	4	4	3	4	4	4	4	5	3	6	5	3	4	4	72-205
Chip Beck	4	3	3	3	4	4	3	4	4	4	5	4	3	4	4	3	4	4	67-206
Jose Maria Olazabal	4	5	4	4	4	4	3	5	4	4	4	3	3	4	4	3	3	4	69-206
Larry Rinker	5	4	4	2	5	4	3	3	4	5	4	4	3	5	4	3	4	4	70-207
Ian Woosnam	4	3	4	2	5	6	5	5	4	4	3	3	3	4	4	3	4	4	70-208
Robert Karlsson	3	4	3	2	5	5	3	4	4	5	4	4	3	4	4	4	5	4	70-208
Malcolm Mackenzie	5	5	3	4	4	4	3	4	5	4	3	4	2	4	4	3	4	5	70-208
Sandy Lyle	4	4	4	3	4	5	3	4	4	4	5	4	3	4	4	3	4	4	70-208
Raymond Floyd	5	4	4	3	5	5	3	5	4	5	4	3	3	5	4	3	4	4	73-208

HOLE SUMMARY

HOLE	PAR	EAGLES	BIRDIES	PARS	BOGEYS	HIGHER	RANK	AVERAGE
1	4	0	1	35	37	2	2	4.53
2	4	0	15	54	6	0	14	3.88
3	4	0	14	56	5	0	14	3.88
4	3	0	14	47	12	2	11	3.03
5	5	1	33	36	5	0	17	4.60
6	4	0	3	46	22	4	5	4.36
7	3	0	4	49	20	2	4	3.28
8	4	1	2	45	23	4	5	4.36
9	5	2	27	35	10	1	16	4.76
OUT	36	4	113	403	140	15		36.68
10	4	0	4	60	11	0	10	4.09
11	4	1	14	50	9	1	12	3.93
12	4	0	10	48	14	3	9	4.15
13	3	0	11	59	5	0	13	2.92
14	4	0	1	32	37	5	1	4.61
15	4	0	5	46	23	1	8	4.27
16	3	0	4	50	20	1	7	3.24
17	5	2	48	24	0	1	18	4.33
18	4	0	1	41	28	5	3	4.49
IN	35	3	98	410	147	17		36.03
TOTAL	71	7	211	813	287	32		72.71

Players Below Par	22
Players At Par	7
Players Above Par	46

LOW SCORES

Low First Nine	Chip Beck	32
Low Second Nine	Jose Maria Olazabal	32
	Ian Woosnam	32
Low Round	Chip Beck	67
	Hale Irwin	67

Conversations with our photographers:
'What magazine are you with?' (below)
'Hello Magazine.'
'Hello!' (right)
'Golf World, more likely.' (above)

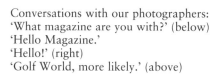

John Cook snapped his tee shot left, out of bounds on No. 9 for double bogey in the final round.

THREE ON VERGE OF MAJOR TITLES

BY ALISTER NICOL

The third day of any 72-hole tournament is frequently referred to by the players themselves as 'moving day.' The third round is the one in which those playing catch-up on the leader have to make their forward press. Day Three of the 121st Open Championship was no different. Before the day was out, more than a few of those following in Nick Faldo's slipstream were praying for some divine intervention from the golfing gods to halt the tall Englishman's seemingly inexorable march to a third Open Championship.

One young man in the chasing pack shared more than the same height — 6 feet, 3 inches — with the halfway leader.

Ernie Els proved he could play on this level.

Like Faldo, young South African Ernie Els has totally dedicated himself to golf and in the opinion of many is the best bet to become South Africa's next superstar, the best since Gary Player.

After opening rounds of 66, 69, the youngster with the power, precision and warm personality of a young Greg Norman shared sixth place with Americans Raymond Floyd and Donnie Hammond. They were one stroke behind Steve Pate, who in turn trailed home-hope Gordon Brand, Jr., and yet another US invader, John Cook, who were three adrift of Faldo, perched atop the leaderboard after a rampaging second-round 64. It was a new experience for Els, whose only previous Open appearance was as an amateur at Troon in 1989. He failed to survive the halfway cut. He has come a long, long way since then and

arrived at Muirfield with an impressive pedigree.

In a sparkling run between January and the middle of February Ernie proved he really was Something Els. He did not shoot over par once in 24 tournament rounds. Three 72s were his highest scores as he compiled a searing stroke average of 68.6. In a five-event run beginning with the South African Open, he was first, first, third, second then first again. That burst of brilliance saw him become the first since his hero, Player, more than a decade ago, to win South Africa's Big Three majors — the South African Open, PGA and Masters titles. It goes without saying he topped the South African Order of Merit and thus gained an exemption from qualifying for Muirfield.

A scratch player since he was 14, Els first became fascinated with golf when he trailed his father round the course in the Easter Transvaal town of Nelspruit. Yet the year he achieved scratch handicap status, he came close to turning his back on the game.

A tall, strong, good-looking all-around sportsman, Els played cricket for his school first team the summer he became a scratch golfer and in the winter wore the No. 8 jersey in the senior rugby side. Ernie also won the Easter Transvaal tennis title that year and was forced into making the choice between tennis and golf as a career. He opted for golf, he told South African writer Ted Partridge, because he felt he was better at it and because he enjoyed it more. 'It is more of a personal challenge,' Els said. 'You play against yourself and the course. If you play a great round like a 64 or 65 you can claim it as a personal achievement.'

Els has already achieved plenty, but there is more to come, much more according to David Feherty, Ireland's highly perceptive Ryder Cup player. The imaginative Ulsterman was one of the few people to better big Ernie during his spectacular run of success last winter. Els placed third in the Bells Cup which Feherty won. Said Feherty at the time, 'Here is a young player who will make some incredible ripples in the world of golf this year and next. He is a player of the future.'

The young Springbok has already taken his talents round the globe. He has played on America's Ben Hogan Tour, has already won enough money to ensure his card on the 1993 PGA European Tour and will play in Australia this coming winter. Sound judges of the golf swing, such as Scotland's Bob Torrance, insist that Ernie will be in golf's fast lane for a long time to come. Torrance said after his first look at the youngster in Cornwall this year, 'Mark my words, that is golf's next superstar.'

On moving day at Muirfield, Els shot 70, his third sub-par score of the week, and while he advanced from seven to eight under par for the championship, he could only shake his head in admiration as the phenomenal Faldo, with 69, went to 14 under par.

A measure of Els' maturity was that another youngster hailed as a star of the future, John Daly, failed miserably to cope with conditions which were far from being as fiendish as Muirfield has unleashed in past Opens. The USPGA champion had 10 sand shots and twice needed two attempts to extricate himself from what five-time Open winner Tom Watson had warned on the eve of the championship were Muirfield's 'inescapable bunkers.'

Daly's move was backwards. He ended up last of the 75 qualifiers.

At age 26, Spain's Jose Maria Olazabal is only a couple of months older than Daly, but as far as success, maturity and golfing wisdom are concerned, Olazabal is light years ahead.

The one thing absent from Olazabal's impressive *curriculum vitae* is a major title. Surely it can only be a matter of time before he puts that kink in his record straight. While Daly applied reverse thrust on moving day, 'Chemma,' the Spanish diminutive for Jose Maria, put the pedal to the metal in the third round, scorching home in 32 for 69, which put him merely six strokes behind.

Winner of 17 professional events, including the 1990 World Series of Golf which he won by a staggering 12 shots from Lanny Wadkins after a record-shattering opening 61, Olazabal has so far earned in excess of £2 million in seven years as a professional. Not winning a major hurts the bachelor from Fuenterrabia in Spain's Basque territory much more deeply than he cares to admit publicly. 'But one year …,' he said. 'I would not want to die before I did.'

Following the first-ever European Ryder Cup success on American soil at Muirfield Village in 1987, US captain Jack Nicklaus said of the talented Olazabal, 'I know it is not physically possible, but that kid has an old head on young shoulders.'

The disbelieving Golden Bear had good reason for voicing his admiration of the 21-year-old baby of Tony Jacklin's team. Because of Olazabal's tender years, Jacklin elected to pair him with celebrated countryman Severiano Ballesteros. The idea was that Seve's vast experience would help nurse the new boy through the cauldron of Ryder Cup competition. Things did not go exactly to plan.

Against Ben Crenshaw and Payne Stewart, in the second-day foursomes, Ballesteros did not play at all well. Olazabal was in great form. When Ballesteros dumped their approach to the final green into a horrible lie in a greenside bunker, the junior member of the team executed a brilliant recovery, leaving Ballesteros an eight-foot, downhill putt. After he had clambered out of the sand, the youngster then had the temerity to tell Seve what to do. 'I told him we had two putts for a win,' Olazabal said, 'and just to touch the ball, just leave it close.'

Whether it was Ryder Cup nerves, whether it was being taken aback by an upstart telling him what he must do, whether it was just a bad putt, nobody will know. But Seve ran his attempt eight feet past. That left Olazabal facing the kind of putt anyone would be excused for missing. He holed it, and Ballesteros almost leapt into his arms.

Since then Olazabal, the only person ever to have won the British Boys, Youths and Amateur titles, has known nothing but success — except in major championships.

However, Olazabal is always prepared to learn. A couple of years ago, he exhausted himself making eight tiring trans-Atlantic trips in a season. Now he paces himself better. Indeed, he took three weeks off before Muirfield, going shopping in San Sebastian with his mother and taking a nephew on frequent visits to the movies.

Golf's most eligible bachelor has few regrets. One of them is the lack of a social life. He says, 'It is not a problem finding a girl, but it is a problem to find a girlfriend. Usually I only have about 20 days at home in the winter.'

Unlike Olazabal, American John Cook turned professional, married and started a family while still in his early 20s, and said after he moved to within four shots of the third-day lead with 70, that perhaps it was all too soon. In common with so many college youngsters both before and since, Cook's appearance on the professional scene saw him heralded as the 'new Nicklaus.' Coming from Jack's university, Ohio State, added an extra burden.

His career had barely started when he ran into some hand problems, which stayed with him for years before an operation in 1989 plucked an offending piece of broken bone. Since then his career has blossomed and, twice a winner on the US Tour early in 1992, perhaps the best is yet to come.

Cook fell in love with the Muirfield galleries who were particularly supportive of him on the third day when he was in the pairing with Faldo. 'Today I learned the British fans know their golf,' Cook said. 'I wish I could import them home.'

A name even less well known than Cook's to the millions watching on television sets round the world on moving day was that of 23-year-old Scot Paul Lawrie. He was paired with Ian Baker-Finch and outscored the defending champion 68 to 72. Lawrie is in his rookie year on the European Tour, having cut his teeth on Scotland's Tartan Tour. He said later, 'What an honour and an education it was to play with Ian. He is a real gentleman and the way he said a few things I knew he wanted me to do well in front of the Scottish crowd. I will never meet a nicer person.'

Baker-Finch said of Lawrie, 'He is strong, he is good, he obviously wants to learn, and he will be around for a long time.'

Jose Maria Olazabal could add the Open Championship to his Boys, Youths and Amateur titles.

When all seemed to have slipped from his grip, Nick Faldo (272) played the game as only a few gifted men have played it.

THE BEST GOLFER OF HIS TIME?

BY ROBERT SOMMERS

A short time after he completed his third round, John Cook took a cold look at his prospects. With a 54-hole score of 203, he lay four strokes behind Nick Faldo, who had matched his own record of 199 for three rounds. Did Cook believe he could catch up? Well, yes and no.

'Nick can be beaten,' Cook said, 'because golf is such a crazy game, but if there is anyone who doesn't beat himself, it is Nick Faldo. He is kind of tough. He's playing so well you just cannot see him making bogeys. But strange things happen. So many times you just hang in there, don't put yourself in positions you don't want to be in by taking unnecessary chances, and take advantage of your opportunities.'

All of that was true, of course. Faldo could be beaten, in fact had been several times earlier in the year, but at the same time he projected overwhelming confidence and the kind of dominance we hadn't seen since the days of Nicklaus. When he held such a substantial lead as he held here, not only *he* expected himself to win, the other players expected it as well.

Steve Pate, who shared second place with Cook, expressed the respect the players felt for Faldo by saying, 'I don't know anyone I'd want to give a four-stroke lead, and Nick Faldo probably least of all. He is the least likely to go out and shoot 74.'

At the same time, those who looked closely at Faldo's recent record had questions if not doubts. Those questions would arise as the Open reached its climax. In recent months he had shown a tendency to play shoddy golf in the last round. In the Irish Open, for example, which was played in early June, Nick

HRH the Duke of York joined the applause.

had led by a similar four strokes going into the final round, and won only after a prolonged play-off. Three weeks later he led the French Open by five strokes going into the last round, gave away all his strokes, and fell to third place at the finish.

Before the last round of the Open ended, his lead, which had seemed so safe, would evaporate as three challengers put enormous pressure on him, first Pate, who was paired with him, and then Cook, who overtook him and came so close to winning it all, and there at the end Jose Maria Olazabal, so far behind when the day began and so close at the end.

Their refusal to yield until the very end created such tension that at times it seemed unbearable, until, after he had won, Faldo's reserve burst and he cried, spilling tears of relief that the dreadful stress had ended.

Seldom has a championship meant so much to a man as this meant to Faldo. His whole being seemed focused on this day and this championship. The battle utterly drained him.

He weathered a day full of strain and frustration, not only from the unrelenting torture of fighting off his challengers, but also from the struggle to right his own shaky game, until at the end, when it all seemed to have slipped from his grip, he played the game as only a few gifted men have played it.

The battle won, he barely heard the applause.

The frustration and strain began from the first shot. Dressed in light blue shirt and vest, in contrast to the royal purple of the previous day, Faldo began by driving to the one place you shouldn't — into the

Faldo drove into a bunker and bogeyed No. 1.

At No. 2, he took par from 30 feet in the rain.

fairway bunker. It cost him a stroke and cut his lead to three over Pate, but he still led Cook by four, because John had bogeyed the opening hole as well.

The day began under warm, sunny skies and the same wind coming from the west, but the usual grey overcast settled over Muirfield just after Faldo and Pate drove on the second. Rain began falling softly at first, then turned into a downpour. Before they played their approaches, both Faldo and Pate stood in mid-fairway slipping into their rain gear while spectators huddled under umbrellas, or dashed to shelter in the exhibition tent nearby. While the rain may have made them uncomfortable, it chased few away. Nor did it mute their cheering when Faldo holed his second putt for his par 4. The rain soon stopped and fell only occasionally through the rest of the day, never again disturbing play.

Meantime, playing a hole in front of Faldo and Pate, Cook made his first move. After an indifferent sand wedge to the third, in pouring rain he hydro-planed his ball 30 feet across the green and into the cup for a birdie 3. He was 10 under par for the 57 holes. Two holes later, he moved even closer.

Cook hadn't hit a fairway through the first three holes, but after a sound par 3 on the fourth, he drove into good position on the fifth, and from well over 200 yards spanked a five iron 15 feet from the cup. He holed the putt for an eagle 3, and now he stood at 12 under par, just one stroke behind Faldo.

The tension grew with every stroke, especially in view of Faldo's game. Nick had shown a little loose-ness, particularly in his approaches. While his drives had put him in good positions, he had left himself 30 feet from the cup on the first, 30 feet on the second, 50 feet on the third, and he missed the green on the fourth. He had made his pars, though, on every hole but the first, and now after another excellent drive, he misplayed his approach to the fifth.

Faldo had driven longer than Cook and had just a six iron left, but he pulled it. His ball plunged into the left greenside bunker and buried in the soft sand, so close to the steep front face he couldn't take a proper stance. After an agonizing number of experiments, he stood with his right foot in the sand and his left knee pressed in a kneeling position against the bunker's face.

From there he had so little hope of playing toward the hole, his par 5 was actually a good score.

While Nick had been foundering, Pate had been playing another erratic round — par on the first, bogey on the second, birdie on the third, bogey on the fourth, and now another birdie on the fifth. When he birdied the sixth he had pulled to within two strokes of Faldo.

It was clear by then that Faldo was not at his best. He had not birdied a hole — indeed, he hadn't been within range of a birdie through five holes — and Pate had outdriven him badly on the sixth, by perhaps 50 yards. Where Nick had played a six iron under a slightly stronger wind the previous day, he needed a two iron here. He couldn't have asked for a better result; his ball bounded onto the green and coasted hole high no more than 15 feet right of the pin. Then he missed the putt. Life was becoming difficult.

Another 15-footer grazed the cup on the seventh, where he made his sixth straight par. Not only were his approaches shaky, but his putting was no better. When he put himself within birdie range, they wouldn't fall as they had in those first two glorious rounds.

Just then he was given a reprieve. After his eagle on the fifth, Cook had bogeyed the seventh with a badly played three iron, and after a sound par 4 on the eighth, he moved on to the ninth, where he had eagled in the third round. Another birdie there and he would climb within a stroke of Faldo once again.

The stone wall most noticeable near the green runs the length of the ninth hole. Possibly trying to put too much into his drive, Cook snapped his ball left. Never gaining much height, it barely cleared the wall. He had driven out of bounds and lost two strokes. Playing a second ball, Cook then drove into the right rough, ruining his chances of reaching the green with his fourth shot, and pitched to 15 feet with his fifth. His putt for the bogey hung on the lip but wouldn't fall.

Cook had made 7 and dropped back to nine under par. He stood four strokes behind Faldo with only nine holes to play. His gallery gave up hope.

With 73, Steve Pate (276) dropped to fourth place.

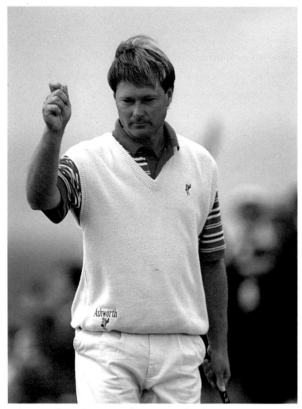

John Cook said, 'I was alive, I was dead, I was really alive, and then pretty much dead.'

With Cook out of the way, Faldo had another stroke of good luck. While he was making his par on the ninth and turning for home in 37, one over standard figures, Pate was stumbling almost as badly as Cook. He made 6. Now Faldo led by three strokes over Pate, and by four over Cook and, surprisingly, Olazabal, who had played through the 12th.

Olazabal had begun the day at 206, seven under par, and had matched par 36 on the first nine, missing four short putts, two leading to bogeys, on the first five holes. Then he began to play the kind of golf everyone expects of him. A sound par on the 10th, then two quick birdies on the 11th and 12th dropped him to nine under par. If he could continue flying his approaches at the flagsticks and holing the putts, he might have a chance.

For any of them to have a hope, though, Faldo would have to crack. Although he wasn't playing at his best, he had been grinding out his pars while others around him had stumbled, and so a Faldo collapse didn't seem likely.

And then what had been seen as a ceremonial round, a sort of walk-over, turned into a wrenching emotional trial.

A deft five iron to the 10th had left Nick 10 feet from the birdie that might have torn the hearts from his challengers. Again, the ball wouldn't fall.

Now Nick made a major mistake. From a position in the 11th fairway that couldn't have been better, he yanked his pitch into the left greenside bunker. After a recovery no closer than 20 feet, he bogeyed. Over 11 holes he had lost two strokes to par, and he hadn't birdied a hole. Now, with seven holes to play, he stood at 12 under par, with both Pate and now Cook within two strokes and Olazabal only three behind.

Finding Cook so close was a major surprise. After his double-bogey 7 at the ninth, John had steadied himself, and even though he missed both the fairway and the green of the 10th, he holed a breaking putt from five or six feet to save one par, then saved another from the rear bunker of the 11th. Still nine under, he holed a breaking 12-footer on the 12th and slipped to 10 under par, back in the hunt.

Faldo moved easily through the 12th, although his loosely played approach once again rolled dangerously close to the left edge leading down into the cave-like bunkers. Nick had been lucky there, but his luck didn't hold on the 13th, the treacherous little 159-yard par 3 protected by steep-walled pot bunkers.

With the hole set on the left no more than 12 or 13 feet from the edge, Faldo played another indifferent iron that barely clung to the right front of the green. Another foot shorter and it would have turned away and scampered down the hill. From about 30 feet, Faldo hit a timid putt that stopped four or five feet short, and his second nibbled at the edge of the hole but wouldn't fall. More than that, it rolled a foot and a half past; he had work to do to save a bogey. The putt did fall, though, and now Faldo, the man who doesn't give away strokes, had given up two in three holes.

The agony hadn't stopped yet. From the 14th tee, Faldo pushed his drive. Watching it dive into the high-faced bunker, Nick bared his teeth, as if he had been stricken with a great pain, for it was certain he could not reach the green, and he lost another stroke.

While Faldo foundered, Cook returned to his early form. His driver functioning again, he had dropped a seven iron within six feet on the 15th and holed it while Faldo was three-putting the 13th, and rolled in a 20-footer on the 16th.

Now Cook stood 12 under par with only the 17th and 18th to play, one of them a near-certain birdie. Suddenly, from a commanding lead of four strokes when the round began, Faldo had fallen to second place, two strokes behind, a swing of six strokes.

The complexion of the Open had changed so quickly and so completely, it was hard to believe Faldo had little chance to win, for that is how the situation looked. Now Faldo would have to play four demanding holes in par to keep up with Olazabal, who had finished by then with 68 and a 72-hole score of 274. Pate was hanging on at nine under, for he had bogeyed the 14th as well.

Faldo would have to assume Cook would birdie the 17th. John had eagled it in the first round and followed with birdies in the second and third. He would certainly birdie there.

Among the qualities that separate the great players from the rest, their refusal to be beaten stands above all else. It manifests itself most notably on the big occasions, with championships of international scope at stake. Somehow they find a way to win, just as the lesser player will find a way to lose. We were about to see an example. With the crowd ready to hand Cook the trophy, Faldo refused to give in.

Surveying what to everyone else seemed a hopeless cause, Faldo figuratively shook himself by the throat and told himself, 'You had better play the best four holes of your life.'

That settled, he split the 15th fairway with his drive and followed with an approach that was mostly skill and partly luck. With the hole still playing into the wind, Faldo softened a five iron that fell well short of the green, then rolled and rolled, and just when we thought it would stop, it crept ever and ever closer. He had played a glorious shot under intense emotional stress that died less than three feet from the cup. Back to 11 under par, a stroke behind Cook. But would it be enough, for Cook by now had ripped a three iron onto the 17th green 30 feet from the cup.

Muirfield's 17th has been a critical hole in three of its last four Opens now, changing the final result in

Jose Maria Olazabal (68—274) played well enough to win, but was let down by his putting.

1972 and 1987, and now again in 1992. Tony Jacklin had the 1972 Open in his hands when Lee Trevino overshot the green with his fourth shot while Jacklin's ball lay only a few feet away for a certain birdie. From the slope behind the green, Trevino chipped in for a par 5, and Jacklin three-putted. Trevino won. Paul Azinger needed only two pars to win in 1987, but he drove into a fairway bunker and bogeyed; then, with a chance to tie Faldo, who had played Muirfield in 18 pars, he bogeyed the 18th as well. The same drama was about to take place with Cook.

Cook had been holing everything he looked at on the home nine, and there was no reason to believe he

Cook had an eagle putt at No. 17 from 30 feet, then a birdie putt just over two feet, before taking par 5.

might not hole this. He did, in fact, play a marvellous putt that looked as if it might fall, then broke away.

No matter; it rolled no more than two feet past. Cook would surely birdie. He had noticed how the ball had swerved away from the hole, and he played for a slight break. He borrowed too much; instead of falling, the ball rimmed the left lip and ran a foot or so past. The gallery gasped, for now Faldo could catch him with a birdie and force a play-off.

With no hesitation, Cook stepped up to his ball once more, and nearly missed again. The ball swirled around inside the cup before it fell. A par 5 where he needed a birdie. Tight-lipped, he strode to the 18th tee.

Behind him, Faldo had saved a par 3 after over-shooting the 16th, then struck a rock-solid four iron onto the 17th green about 10 feet closer than Cook's ball had been. An eagle was not out of the question, and the birdie seemed certain.

Cook, meantime, had driven straight down the 18th fairway, in prime position for his shot into the green. Now, though, he faced a dilemma. His ball lay about 200 yards from the green, ordinarily three-iron distance for him, but with the wind in his face, John felt he needed a two iron.

As Faldo studied his putt, a nervous murmur spread through the gallery, now packed five and six deep around the green.

'Cook's missed the green,' someone whispered.

At No. 18, Cook hit a two iron into the gallery, took a drop without penalty, pitched on to 10 feet and bogeyed.

'He's hit it in the crowd,' another added.

Indeed he had. Indecisive about his choice of clubs, Cook had flinched coming into the ball. It shot off to the right and bounced into the gallery bunched behind the iron fences the R and A uses to hold the galleries in check.

He was given a drop without penalty, pitched on about 10 feet past the hole, and missed the putt. A bogey 5; he had shot 70 and slipped to 11 under par, with 273. Now Faldo had his opening.

With an eagle beckoning, Faldo hit a weak, tentative putt that pulled up a foot or so short. No matter; the birdie fell, and Nick had surged to the front once again. Now only a par at the 18th and he would be champion again.

He made a cast-iron 4. His drive couldn't have been better, and his three iron looked as if it might rattle the flagstick. The ball carried over the top of the pin and ran off the back edge of the green. His putt looked at first as if it might leave him five or six feet short, but on a slick green it edged ever closer to the cup, swung away as it drew close, and pulled up within easy holing distance.

Faldo rolled the ball in, then bent over to pick it from the cup. When he straightened, he couldn't raise his head. This supposedly aloof man showed he had a soul. All the teeming emotion he had held within himself through this long and trying day had finally welled up and broken out.

His face twisted as if in pain, he took control of himself long enough to raise both arms to the gallery, then turned and walked off the green, still overwhelmed by his own accomplishment.

This was a scene we hadn't seen before. We would have to go back to Bobby Jones at Hoylake 62 years earlier for a similar moment, when that great man had needed both his hands to hold onto a drink while he waited for Mac Smith to play those last agonizing holes.

We have known of nothing like this from the other great champions who followed, cold men like Ben Hogan and Jack Nicklaus, happy men like Tom Watson, and certainly not from Arnold Palmer, to whom golf is such a joy. Evidently Faldo is different.

Reaching the back of the green, he bent over his

Faldo had his left knee against the bunker's face at No. 5, as he played out to 30 feet and made par 5 with two putts.

In the midst of his struggle, he three-putted at No. 13.

golf bag, still choked with emotion, then walked to the scorer's room, where he would check his card. Once inside, he broke down again; he laid his head on the shoulder of David Begg, the Open's press officer, and sobbed.

This was a new vision of the man. We had seen finally what this game meant to him, the immense dedication that had driven him to reach the very top of the game. Nick Faldo may be the best golfer of his time.

Faldo (above) pushed his drive at No. 14 into a steep bunker. He could not reach the green, and made a bogey to fall two strokes behind.

Faldo (below) told himself, 'You had better play the best four holes of your life.' He then drove well at No. 15, and hit probably his best shot of the week, a soft five iron that rolled to within three feet of the hole to set up a birdie.

Faldo (above left) saved par after over-shooting the green at No. 16. Knowing that Cook had cleared the way with a closing bogey, Faldo (left) two-putted for birdie at No. 17 to regain the lead. His second shot at No. 18 (above), with a three iron, was on line to the flagstick but ran to the back edge of the green.

It seemed at first that Faldo's putt might be short, but it kept rolling on the slick green, settling one foot from the hole.

FOURTH ROUND RESULTS

HOLE	1	2	3	4	5	6	7	8	9	10	11	12	13	14	15	16	17	18	
PAR	4	4	4	3	5	4	3	4	5	4	4	4	3	4	4	3	5	4	TOTAL
Nick Faldo	5	4	4	3	5	4	3	4	5	4	5	4	4	5	3	3	4	4	73-272
John Cook	5	4	3	3	3	4	4	4	7	4	4	3	3	4	3	2	5	5	70-273
Jose Maria Olazabal	5	3	4	4	5	4	3	4	4	4	3	3	3	4	4	3	4	4	68-274
Steve Pate	4	5	3	4	4	3	3	4	6	4	4	4	3	5	6	3	4	4	73-276
Andrew Magee	4	4	4	3	3	4	3	4	4	4	4	4	3	5	4	3	5	5	70-279
Malcolm Mackenzie	4	4	5	2	4	4	4	4	4	4	5	4	3	4	4	4	4	4	71-279
Robert Karlsson	5	4	4	3	5	4	3	4	7	4	4	4	2	4	4	2	4	4	71-279
Ian Woosnam	4	4	4	3	5	5	4	3	4	5	3	4	4	3	5	4	2	4	4	71-279
Gordon Brand, Jr.	4	4	4	4	4	5	3	4	5	4	4	5	2	5	5	5	4	3	74-279
Donnie Hammond	3	5	3	3	5	5	3	4	6	5	5	4	3	4	4	3	4	4	74-279
Ernie Els	5	5	4	3	6	3	4	4	6	4	3	4	3	5	3	3	4	5	74-279

HOLE SUMMARY

HOLE	PAR	EAGLES	BIRDIES	PARS	BOGEYS	HIGHER	RANK	AVERAGE
1	4	0	3	33	30	9	1	4.60
2	4	0	18	46	11	0	15	3.91
3	4	0	13	57	5	0	16	3.89
4	3	0	10	47	17	1	9	3.12
5	5	4	43	24	4	0	18	4.37
6	4	0	9	42	23	1	7	4.21
7	3	0	6	43	23	3	3	3.31
8	4	0	2	60	12	1	9	4.16
9	5	0	15	46	11	3	13	5.03
OUT	36	4	119	398	136	18		36.60
10	4	0	4	49	22	0	6	4.24
11	4	0	12	52	10	1	14	4.00
12	4	0	10	47	17	1	12	4.12
13	3	0	3	60	11	1	8	3.13
14	4	0	2	34	36	3	2	4.53
15	4	0	4	43	24	4	5	4.37
16	3	0	9	51	13	2	11	3.11
17	5	0	39	33	2	1	17	4.53
18	4	0	4	41	27	3	4	4.39
IN	35	0	87	410	162	16		36.42
TOTAL	71	4	206	808	298	34		73.02

			LOW SCORES		
Players Below Par	8				
Players At Par	10	**Low First Nine**	Andrew Magee	33
			Greg Norman	33
Players Above Par	57			
		Low Second Nine	Robert Karlsson	32
			Jose Maria Olazabal	32
		Low Round	Ian Baker-Finch	68
			Greg Norman	68
			Jose Maria Olazabal	68

CHAMPIONSHIP HOLE SUMMARY

HOLE	PAR	EAGLES	BIRDIES	PARS	BOGEYS	HIGHER	RANK	AVERAGE
1	4	0	13	243	175	31	1	4.49
2	4	0	82	325	55	0	14	3.94
3	4	0	92	346	23	1	16	3.85
4	3	0	67	321	68	6	11	3.03
5	5	21	234	178	28	1	18	4.47
6	4	0	47	293	114	8	9	4.18
7	3	1	32	309	107	13	4	3.22
8	4	1	38	298	115	10	6	4.21
9	5	8	130	266	46	12	15	4.84
OUT	36	31	735	2579	731	82		36.23
10	4	0	41	297	118	6	7	4.19
11	4	1	70	320	66	5	13	4.01
12	4	0	46	318	88	10	10	4.14
13	3	0	50	360	51	1	12	3.01
14	4	0	20	222	197	23	1	4.49
15	4	0	37	295	122	8	5	4.22
16	3	0	39	327	90	6	8	3.14
17	5	12	235	201	10	4	17	4.48
18	4	0	22	265	153	22	3	4.38
IN	35	13	560	2605	895	85		36.06
TOTAL	71	44	1295	5184	1626	167		72.29

	FIRST ROUND	SECOND ROUND	THIRD ROUND	FOURTH ROUND	TOTAL
Players Below Par	56	46	22	8	132
Players At Par	24	24	7	10	65
Players Above Par	76	86	46	57	265

ATTENDANCE

PRACTICE ROUNDS	25,897
FIRST ROUND	27,431
SECOND ROUND	32,874
THIRD ROUND	31,731
FOURTH ROUND	29,847
TOTAL	146,427

Faldo was overcome by emotion when the victory finally was his.

A VICTORY WORTH CRYING ABOUT

BY JOHN HOPKINS

Nick Faldo had always said he wanted people to say they had seen him play golf in the way that people say they saw Olivier act or heard Mario Lanza sing and anyone who was at Muirfield on the fourth day of the Open Championship is not likely to forget the sight of Faldo going from probable victory to likely defeat and rising again to claim a magnificent victory. No wonder he cried. It was, as Peter Alliss remarked, as if he had pulled the rabbit out of a top hat, lost it and found it in time to bring his conjuring act to its conclusion.

Faldo's victory confirmed him as the best British golfer of all time, better than Sir Henry Cotton, who also won three Opens. Faldo is a more accomplished player, even than Harry Vardon, who held seven major titles but only one from the United States. Faldo won the Masters in 1989 and 1990. It confirmed what had already been known: that since Faldo won his first major, at Muirfield in July 1987, he has been the man to beat in major championships, the one name most likely to be mentioned in any poll of pre-tournament favourites.

From 1987 to the day after this Open there had been 23 major championships. Faldo has won five of them. Furthermore, he finished second to Curtis Strange in the 1988 US Open and third in the 1990 US Open. No other golfer has approached Faldo's success rate in this time span, first or second in every third major championship. Indeed, only Payne Stewart and Strange have won more than one major title since the start of 1987.

Faldo has a rage to succeed, a desire to triumph over golf, one of the most fiendish of all games, which is not unlike John McEnroe's at tennis. Down the years one golfer after another has attempted to master the unpredictabilities of golf, and while some have got close, none has succeeded for any length of time.

Ben Hogan found that there was always one part of his game that would be in disrepair even though the rest of his game was humming and whirring smoothly. Tom Watson sought to hit the perfect golf shot and achieved it at times but not as often as he wanted. Jack Nicklaus brought great powers of concentration, determination and thoroughness to the game, which, when allied to his near-genius for playing, made him the most complete player the game had seen. But none of them ever mastered golf for more than a few fleeting moments at any given time.

Trying to swing a golf club with a shaft that twists, turns, vibrates and generates more than one ton at impact is something that can only be repeated accurately in a laboratory. A golf course may be used *as a* laboratory, but this is not to say it *is* a laboratory. It is hard to imagine anywhere less like a laboratory, in fact.

For years, though, Faldo tried to succeed where others failed. It was as if he was put on this earth to attempt to do something at which no one else had succeeded. He always wanted to win; he always wanted to be the best; he always wanted to know how something worked. George and Joyce Faldo gave their son — and only child — a bicycle as a birthday present. The first thing Nick did with it was strip it down to see how it worked.

When these internal demons coincided, as they did when he took up golf, then the sparks were going to fly. 'I never worried about Nick not making a success of being a professional because so many people told me how good he was,' his mother has said. Faldo has often spoken of his desire to be able to hit a golf ball so accurately it would deviate no more than a couple of feet either side of its target. And there have been times lately when he has achieved that remarkable standard.

It is when he has not been able to achieve this degree of precision that Faldo's troubles have begun. His is a rage to succeed, as I have said, a desire to reproduce again and again the shots he knows he is capable of playing. McEnroe's outbursts at umpires and line judges, sometimes truly awful in their vulgar courseness, are mirrored by Faldo's mutterings after a shot has failed to land on precisely the spot of turf he had selected. If you could hear what Faldo was saying at such times, your ears would burn.

But lately, he has begun to realize that even he cannot reproduce the perfect or even near-perfect shot as often as he would like or feels capable of and a new attitude was needed. The anger he directed at himself when a shot was as little as one degree off line caused more errors. It was time to change his attitude and in casting around for one, he noticed Freddie Couples' behaviour on the 14th green at Augusta earlier this year. There was genuine admiration in Faldo's voice when he talked two months later of the way Couples coped with a double bogey at a key moment during the Masters.

'It came at precisely the wrong time and I thought, "Right, he's had it. He's gone,"' Faldo said. 'But he hadn't. He approached it with exactly the right attitude. He gave this impression of being able to forget all about it. It was as if he had said to himself, "It's happened, so let's forget it and get on with the rest of the round." He picked himself up and made me realize that was the best way to approach setbacks. That was a big lesson, the biggest since I started trying to be lighter on myself.'

Another lesson was learned when he read a book called *Being Happy*. It brought home to Faldo that he needed to smooth off a few rough edges for himself as much as for others — and perhaps most of all for his two young children. 'Kids are great, aren't they,' he says. 'They don't know what is going on. All they know is I'm their father and they want to jump all over me when they want to. It puts it all into perspective, doesn't it?'

Learning these truths and slowly being able to put them into practice enabled Faldo to embark on a scoring sequence in tournaments in the US and Europe this season that takes some beating. It is worth looking at closely.

Starting in the Johnnie Walker Asian Classic in the Far East, he played 58 rounds including his four at Muirfield. He was under par in 45 of them and level par in four. This means that while challenging some of the world's best courses — Bay Hill, the stadium course used for The Players Championship at Jacksonville, Augusta National, the West Course at Wentworth, Pebble Beach and, finally, Muirfield — Faldo was only over par in nine rounds. His cumulative total was 128 under par.

In 10 events on the European Tour, his worst finish was 20th in Thailand at the start of the season. From The Players Championship in March to the Open Championship he competed in 12 events and finished in the top eight in 11 of them and 13th in the other one. From the Dunhill British Masters in June to the Open five weeks later he went fourth, first (Irish Open), fourth (US Open), third (French Open), third (Scottish Open) and first.

The manner of Faldo's victory was not only perfectly in keeping with the Muirfield tradition that makes Opens at this lovely course on the banks of the Firth of Forth the benchmarks of golfing history. It also silenced the doubters, the first refrains of whose doleful chorus were beginning to be heard. Was Faldo's best behind him was a suggestion that was heard on the eve of the Open.

In an article published on the eve of the Open I wrote the following: 'It is true that Faldo has found it harder to come through and win on the fourth day of tournaments this season. This characteristic is a mark of champions and was formerly a strength of Faldo's. He had an outside chance to win at St Mellion in the Benson & Hedges International, the Spanish Open and a good chance to win the Volvo PGA at Wentworth. At Woburn in the British Masters, in the Irish Open and the French Open he was leading with only a few holes to go. This season he has lost tournaments he should have won and, once, won a tournament he should have lost.

'Would the Nick Faldo of former years have won more of these events had he got into the same winning positions? Yes, he probably would. There is no doubt that up to the Open Faldo was less secure mentally than he used to be. He tended to play the occasional rank bad shot when on the verge of victory. You could see he was under pressure.

Having signed his scorecard and regained his composure, Faldo emerged to the thunderous cheers of the crowd.

'If you know what to look for you can spot the telltale signs of Faldo's nervousness. His tongue flicks repeatedly across his lips and on some very important putts his right thumb flutters up and down on the grip of his club like the wings of a moth struggling against a pane of glass. Perhaps such battle scars are not surprising in one who has been so competitive at the highest level for the past five years. After all, Faldo is no longer a young man. He will be 35 on the Saturday of the Open.

'But the former Nick Faldo is not as complete or as steady a player as the current Nick Faldo. The current Nick Faldo may have squandered more chances but the former Nick Faldo would not have created so many winning positions.

'Let us consider Faldo's record in the months preceding the last Open at Muirfield, where he won his first Open, and the equivalent time span before St Andrews in 1990, where he won his second. In 1987, the varying parts that comprised Faldo's remodelled swing finally clicked into place in April. In a tournament in the United States he put together four rounds of 67. He returned to Europe in May and at a teasing Las Brisas course won the Spanish Open with rounds of 72, 71, 71, 72. He finished fifth in the French Open, second in the Belgium and 18th and 21st in the Irish and Scottish Opens. Then he won at Muirfield, the only man not to go over par. His stroke average in Europe prior to that year's Open was 70.02 from 35 rounds.

'What about 1990? He entered seven events before the Open, finished second twice and had two other top-10 finishes but also a 54th in the Dunhill British

Gill and Nick Faldo savoured the victory.

Masters and a joint 12th in the Benson & Hedges. His stroke average for these 28 rounds was 70.25. This year's stroke average from eight events and 24 rounds, up to and including the French Open, is 69.25, so he is almost a stroke better than he was both two years ago and five years ago.'

There was no doubt that Faldo was at the peak of his game when he arrived at Muirfield. One might wish for him to win a major title without a rival missing a short putt but there again, the reason why this happened first to Scott Hoch and then John Cook could be Faldo's mental strength and intimidatory powers.

In victory he cried. He didn't just sniffle, shed the odd tear. He wept, starting the moment his penultimate putt on the 72nd green rolled slowly to within a foot or so of the hole. His knees wobbled, his voice wavered and for half an hour he looked and sounded as though he might break into tears once again.

There is nothing wrong with crying. Big men cry because they are man enough to know they won't be thought any the less of for doing so. Showing such a human side may have been the making of Faldo. Before, he had appeared to be a machine, grinding out par figures one after another, 18 in a row at Muirfield in 1987. Now, he was a hero, a man with blood in his veins and tears in his eyes. He was crying because he had just wretched two birdies from Muirfield's four finishing holes and with them a victory that was as courageous as any ever seen. It was something to cry about. It was also something to shout about.

'From almost a disaster to the absolute ultimate,' Faldo truly had won the Open Championship his way.

Defending Open champion Ian Baker-Finch was in joint 19th place with 68 in the final round.

RECORDS OF THE OPEN CHAMPIONSHIP

MOST VICTORIES
6, Harry Vardon, 1896-98-99-1903-11-14
5, James Braid, 1901-05-06-08-10; J.H. Taylor, 1894-95-1900-09-13; Peter Thomson, 1954-55-56-58-65; Tom Watson, 1975-77-80-82-83

MOST TIMES RUNNER-UP OR JOINT RUNNER-UP
7, Jack Nicklaus, 1964-67-68-72-76-77-79
6, J.H. Taylor, 1896-1904-05-06-07-14

OLDEST WINNER
Old Tom Morris, 46 years 99 days, 1867
Roberto de Vicenzo, 44 years 93 days, 1967

YOUNGEST WINNER
Young Tom Morris, 17 years 5 months 8 days, 1868
Willie Auchterlonie, 21 years 24 days, 1893
Severiano Ballesteros, 22 years 3 months 12 days, 1979

YOUNGEST AND OLDEST COMPETITOR
John Ball, 14 years, 1878
Gene Sarazen, 71 years 4 months 13 days, 1973

BIGGEST MARGIN OF VICTORY
13 strokes, Old Tom Morris, 1862
12 strokes, Young Tom Morris, 1870
8 strokes, J.H. Taylor, 1900 and 1913; James Braid, 1908
6 strokes, Bobby Jones, 1927; Walter Hagen, 1929; Arnold Palmer, 1962; Johnny Miller, 1976

LOWEST WINNING AGGREGATES
268 (68, 70, 65, 65), Tom Watson, Turnberry, 1977
270 (67, 65, 67, 71), Nick Faldo, St Andrews, 1990
271 (68, 70, 64, 69), Tom Watson, Muirfield, 1980
272 (71, 71, 64, 66), Ian Baker-Finch, Royal Birkdale, 1991; (66, 64, 69, 73), Nick Faldo, Muirfield, 1992

LOWEST AGGREGATES BY RUNNER-UP
269 (68, 70, 65, 66), Jack Nicklaus, Turnberry, 1977
273 (66, 67, 70, 70), John Cook, Muirfield, 1992
274 (68, 70, 69, 67), Mike Harwood, Royal Birkdale, 1991
275 (68, 67, 71, 69), Lee Trevino, Muirfield, 1980; (70, 67, 69, 69), Nick Price, Royal Lytham, 1988; (69, 70, 72, 64), Greg Norman, Royal Troon, 1989; (68, 67, 69, 71), Wayne Grady, Royal Troon, 1989; (74, 68, 68, 65), Mark McNulty, St Andrews, 1990; (68, 68, 68, 71), Payne Stewart, St Andrews, 1990

LOWEST AGGREGATE BY AN AMATEUR
283 (74, 70, 71, 68), Guy Wolstenholme, St Andrews, 1960

LOWEST INDIVIDUAL ROUND
63, Mark Hayes, second round, Turnberry, 1977; Isao Aoki, third round, Muirfield, 1980; Greg Norman, second round, Turnberry, 1986; Paul Broadhurst, third round, St Andrews, 1990; Jodie Mudd, fourth round, Royal Birkdale, 1991

LOWEST INDIVIDUAL ROUND BY AN AMATEUR
66, Frank Stranahan, fourth round, Troon, 1950

LOWEST FIRST ROUND
64, Craig Stadler, Royal Birkdale, 1983; Christy O'Connor Jr., Royal St George's, 1985; Rodger Davis, Muirfield, 1987; Raymond Floyd and Steve Pate, Muirfield, 1992

LOWEST SECOND ROUND
63, Mark Hayes, Turnberry, 1977; Greg Norman, Turnberry, 1986

LOWEST THIRD ROUND
63, Isao Aoki, Muirfield, 1980; Paul Broadhurst, St Andrews, 1990

LOWEST FOURTH ROUND
63, Jodie Mudd, Royal Birkdale, 1991

LOWEST FIRST 36 HOLES
130 (66, 64) Nick Faldo, Muirfield, 1992
132 (67, 65) Henry Cotton, Sandwich, 1934; (66, 66) Greg Norman and (67, 65) Nick Faldo, St Andrews, 1990

LOWEST SECOND 36 HOLES
130 (65, 65), Tom Watson, Turnberry, 1977; (64, 66) Ian Baker-Finch, Royal Birkdale, 1991

LOWEST FIRST 54 HOLES
199 (67, 65, 67), Nick Faldo, St Andrews, 1990; (66, 64, 69), Nick Faldo, Muirfield, 1992

LOWEST FINAL 54 HOLES
200 (70, 65, 65), Tom Watson, Turnberry, 1977
201 (71, 64, 66), Ian Baker-Finch, Royal Birkdale, 1991

LOWEST 9 HOLES
28, Denis Durnian, first 9, Royal Birkdale, 1983
29, Peter Thomson and Tom Haliburton, first 9, Royal

Lytham, 1958; Tony Jacklin, first 9, St Andrews, 1970; Bill Longmuir, first 9, Royal Lytham, 1979; David J. Russell, first 9, Royal Lytham, 1988; Ian Baker-Finch and Paul Broadhurst, first 9, St Andrews, 1990; Ian Baker-Finch, first 9, Royal Birkdale, 1991

CHAMPIONS IN THREE DECADES
Harry Vardon, 1896, 1903, 1911
J.H. Taylor, 1894, 1900, 1913
Gary Player, 1959, 1968, 1974

BIGGEST SPAN BETWEEN FIRST AND LAST VICTORIES
19 years, J.H. Taylor, 1894-1913
18 years, Harry Vardon, 1896-1914
15 years, Gary Player, 1959-74
14 years, Henry Cotton, 1934-48

SUCCESSIVE VICTORIES
4, Young Tom Morris, 1868-72. No championship in 1871
3, Jamie Anderson, 1877-79; Bob Ferguson, 1880-82, Peter Thomson, 1954-56
2, Old Tom Morris, 1861-62; J.H. Taylor, 1894-95; Harry Vardon, 1898-99; James Braid, 1905-06; Bobby Jones, 1926-27; Walter Hagen, 1928-29; Bobby Locke, 1949-50; Arnold Palmer, 1961-62; Lee Trevino, 1971-72; Tom Watson, 1982-83

VICTORIES BY AMATEURS
3, Bobby Jones, 1926-27-30
2, Harold Hilton, 1892-97
1, John Ball, 1890
Roger Wethered lost a play-off in 1921

HIGHEST NUMBER OF TOP FIVE FINISHES
16, J.H. Taylor, Jack Nicklaus
15, Harry Vardon, James Braid

HIGHEST NUMBER OF ROUNDS UNDER 70
30, Jack Nicklaus
24, Nick Faldo
23, Tom Watson
21, Lee Trevino
16, Severiano Ballesteros
15, Peter Thomson
14, Gary Player
13, Ben Crenshaw, Bernhard Langer, Greg Norman
12, Bobby Locke, Arnold Palmer
11, Payne Stewart

OUTRIGHT LEADER AFTER EVERY ROUND
Willie Auchterlonie, 1893; J.H. Taylor, 1894 and 1900; James Braid, 1908; Ted Ray, 1912; Bobby Jones, 1927; Gene Sarazen, 1932; Henry Cotton, 1934; Tom Weiskopf, 1973

RECORD LEADS (SINCE 1892)
After 18 holes:
4 strokes, James Braid, 1908; Bobby Jones, 1927; Henry Cotton, 1934; Christy O'Connor Jr., 1985
After 36 holes:
9 strokes, Henry Cotton, 1934
After 54 holes:
10 strokes, Henry Cotton, 1934
7 strokes, Tony Lema, 1964

6 strokes, James Braid, 1908
5 strokes, Arnold Palmer, 1962; Bill Rogers, 1981; Nick Faldo, 1990

CHAMPIONS WITH EACH ROUND LOWER THAN PREVIOUS ONE
Jack White, 1904, Sandwich, 80, 75, 72, 69
James Braid, 1906, Muirfield, 77, 76, 74, 73
Ben Hogan, 1953, Carnoustie, 73, 71, 70, 68
Gary Player, 1959, Muirfield, 75, 71, 70, 68

CHAMPION WITH FOUR ROUNDS THE SAME
Densmore Shute, 1933, St Andrews, 73, 73, 73, 73 (excluding the play-off)

BIGGEST VARIATION BETWEEN ROUNDS OF A CHAMPION
14 strokes, Henry Cotton, 1934, second round 65, fourth round 79
11 strokes, Jack White, 1904, first round 80, fourth round 69; Greg Norman, 1986, first round 74, second round 63, third round 74

BIGGEST VARIATION BETWEEN TWO ROUNDS
17 strokes, Jack Nicklaus, 1981, first round 83, second round 66; Ian Baker-Finch, 1986, first round 86, second round 69

BEST COMEBACK BY CHAMPIONS
After 18 holes:
Harry Vardon, 1896, 11 strokes behind the leader
After 36 holes:
George Duncan, 1920, 13 strokes behind the leader
After 54 holes:
Jim Barnes, 1925, 5 strokes behind the leader
Of non-champions, Greg Norman, 1989, 7 strokes behind the leader and lost in a play-off

CHAMPIONS WITH FOUR ROUNDS UNDER 70
None
Arnold Palmer, 1962, Tom Watson, 1977 and 1980, Severiano Ballesteros, 1984, Mark Calcavecchia, 1989, and Nick Faldo, 1990 and 1992, had three rounds under 70
Of non-champions, Phil Rodgers, 1963, Jack Nicklaus, 1977, Lee Trevino, 1980, Nick Faldo, 1984, Nick Price and Curtis Strange, 1988, Wayne Grady and Tom Watson, 1989, Mark McNulty, Payne Stewart, Ian Woosnam and Greg Norman, 1990, Mike Harwood and Mark O'Meara, 1991, and Jose Maria Olazabal, 1992, had three rounds under 70

BEST FINISHING ROUND BY A CHAMPION
65, Tom Watson, Turnberry, 1977; Severiano Ballesteros, Royal Lytham, 1988
66, Johnny Miller, Royal Birkdale, 1976; Ian Baker-Finch, Royal Birkdale, 1991

WORST FINISHING ROUND BY A CHAMPION SINCE 1920
79, Henry Cotton, Sandwich, 1934
78, Reg Whitcombe, Sandwich, 1938
77, Walter Hagen, Hoylake, 1924

WORST OPENING ROUND BY A CHAMPION SINCE 1919
80, George Duncan, Deal, 1920 (he also had a second round of 80)
77, Walter Hagen, Hoylake, 1924

BEST OPENING ROUND BY A CHAMPION
66, Peter Thomson, Royal Lytham, 1958; Nick Faldo, Muirfield, 1992
67, Henry Cotton, Sandwich, 1934; Tom Watson, Royal Birkdale, 1983; Severiano Ballesteros, Royal Lytham, 1988; Nick Faldo, St Andrews, 1990

BIGGEST RECOVERY IN 18 HOLES BY A CHAMPION
George Duncan, Deal, 1920, was 13 strokes behind the leader, Abe Mitchell, after 36 holes and level after 54

MOST APPEARANCES ON FINAL DAY (SINCE 1892)
30, J.H. Taylor
29, Jack Nicklaus
27, Harry Vardon, James Braid
26, Peter Thomson
25, Gary Player
23, Dai Rees
22, Henry Cotton

CHAMPIONSHIP WITH HIGHEST NUMBER OF ROUNDS UNDER 70
102, Royal Birkdale, 1991

CHAMPIONSHIP SINCE 1946 WITH THE FEWEST ROUNDS UNDER 70
St Andrews, 1946; Hoylake, 1947; Portrush, 1951; Hoylake, 1956; Carnoustie, 1968. All had only two rounds under 70

LONGEST COURSE
Carnoustie, 1968, 7252 yd (6631 m)

COURSES MOST OFTEN USED
St Andrews and Prestwick, (but not since 1925), 24; Muirfield, 14; Sandwich, 11; Hoylake, 10; Royal Lytham, 8; Royal Birkdale, 7; Musselburgh, and Royal Troon, 6; Carnoustie, 5; Deal and Turnberry, 2; Royal Portrush and Prince's, 1

PRIZE MONEY

Year	Total	First Prize
1860	nil	nil
1863	10	nil
1864	16	6
1876	20	20
1889	22	8
1891	28.50	10
1892	110	(Amateur winner)
1893	100	30
1910	125	50
1920	225	75
1927	275	100
1930	400	100
1931	500	100
1946	1,000	150
1949	1,700	300
1953	2,450	500
1954	3,500	750
1955	3,750	1,000
1958	4,850	1,000
1959	5,000	1,000
1960	7,000	1,250
1961	8,500	1,400
1963	8,500	1,500
1965	10,000	1,750
1966	15,000	2,100
1968	20,000	3,000
1969	30,000	4,250
1970	40,000	5,250
1971	45,000	5,500
1972	50,000	5,500
1975	75,000	7,500
1977	100,000	10,000
1978	125,000	12,500
1979	155,000	15,500
1980	200,000	25,000
1982	250,000	32,000
1983	300,000	40,000
1984	451,000	55,000
1985	530,000	65,000
1986	600,000	70,000
1987	650,000	75,000
1988	700,000	80,000
1989	750,000	80,000
1990	825,000	85,000
1991	900,000	90,000
1992	950,000	95,000

ATTENDANCE

Year	Attendance
1962	37,098
1963	24,585
1964	35,954
1965	32,927
1966	40,182
1967	29,880
1968	51,819
1969	46,001
1970	81,593
1971	70,076
1972	84,746
1973	78,810
1974	92,796
1975	85,258
1976	92,021
1977	87,615
1978	125,271
1979	134,501
1980	131,610
1981	111,987
1982	133,299
1983	142,892
1984	193,126
1985	141,619
1986	134,261
1987	139,189
1988	191,334
1989	160,639
1990	208,680
1991	189,435
1992	146,427

Lee Trevino (1971, 1972)   Gary Player (1959, 1968, 1974)   Tom Weiskopf (1973)

Jack Nicklaus (1966, 1970 and 1978) and six times runner-up.

Sandy Lyle (1985)

Greg Norman (1986)

Mark Calcavecchia (1989)

Tom Watson (1975, 1977, 1980, 1982, 1983)

Seve Ballesteros (1979, 1984, 1988)

PAST RESULTS

* Denotes amateurs

1860 PRESTWICK

Willie Park, Musselburgh	55	59	60	174
Tom Morris Sr, Prestwick	58	59	59	176
Andrew Strath, St Andrews				180
Robert Andrew, Perth				191
George Brown, Blackheath				192
Charles Hunter, Prestwick St Nicholas				195

1861 PRESTWICK

Tom Morris Sr, Prestwick	54	56	53	163
Willie Park, Musselburgh	54	54	59	167
William Dow, Musselburgh	59	58	54	171
David Park, Musselburgh	58	57	57	172
Robert Andrew, Perth	58	61	56	175
Peter McEwan, Bruntsfield	56	60	62	178

1862 PRESTWICK

Tom Morris Sr, Prestwick	52	55	56	163
Willie Park, Musselburgh	59	59	58	176
Charles Hunter, Prestwick	60	60	58	178
William Dow, Musselburgh	60	58	63	181
* James Knight, Prestwick	62	61	63	186
* J.F. Johnston, Prestwick	64	69	75	208

1863 PRESTWICK

Willie Park, Musselburgh	56	54	58	168
Tom Morris Sr, Prestwick	56	58	56	170
David Park, Musselburgh	55	63	54	172
Andrew Strath, St Andrews	61	55	58	174
George Brown, St Andrews	58	61	57	176
Robert Andrew, Perth	62	57	59	178

1864 PRESTWICK

Tom Morris Sr, Prestwick	54	58	55	167
Andrew Strath, St Andrews	56	57	56	169
Robert Andrew, Perth	57	58	60	175
Willie Park, Musselburgh	55	67	55	177
William Dow, Musselburgh	56	58	67	181
William Strath, St Andrews	60	62	60	182

1865 Prestwick

Andrew Strath, St Andrews	55	54	53	162
Willie Park, Musselburgh	56	52	56	164
William Dow, Musselburgh				171
Robert Kirk, St Andrews	64	54	55	173
Tom Morris Sr, St Andrews	57	61	56	174
* William Doleman, Glasgow	62	57	59	178

1866 PRESTWICK

Willie Park, Musselburgh	54	56	59	169
David Park, Musselburgh	58	57	56	171
Robert Andrew, Perth	58	59	59	176
Tom Morris Sr, St Andrews	61	58	59	178
Robert Kirk, St Andrews	60	62	58	180

Andrew Strath, Prestwick	61	61	60	182
* William Doleman, Glasgow	60	60	62	182

1867 PRESTWICK

Tom Morris Sr, St Andrews	58	54	58	170
Willie Park, Musselburgh	58	56	58	172
Andrew Strath, St Andrews	61	57	56	174
Tom Morris Jr, St Andrews	58	59	58	175
Robert Kirk, St Andrews	57	60	60	177
*William Doleman, Glasgow	55	66	57	178

1868 PRESTWICK

Tom Morris Jr, St Andrews	50	55	52	157
Robert Andrew, Perth	53	54	52	159
Willie Park, Musselburgh	58	50	54	162
Robert Kirk, St Andrews	56	59	56	171
John Allen, Westward Ho!	54	52	63	172
Tom Morris Sr, St Andrews	56	62	58	176

1869 PRESTWICK

Tom Morris Jr, St Andrews	51	54	49	154
Tom Morris Sr, St Andrews	54	50	53	157
*S. Mure Fergusson, Royal and Ancient	57	54	54	165
Robert Kirk, St Andrews	53	58	57	168
David Strath, St Andrews	53	56	60	169
Jamie Anderson, St Andrews	60	56	57	173

1870 PRESTWICK

Tom Morris Jr, St Andrews	47	51	51	149
Bob Kirk, Royal Blackheath	52	52	57	161
David Strath, St Andrews	54	49	58	161
Tom Morris Sr, St Andrews	56	52	54	162
*William Doleman, Musselburgh	57	56	58	171
Willie Park, Musselburgh	60	55	58	173

1871 NO COMPETITION

1872 PRESTWICK

Tom Morris Jr, St Andrews	57	56	53	166
David Strath, St Andrews	56	52	61	169
*William Doleman, Musselburgh	63	60	54	177
Tom Morris Sr, St Andrews	62	60	57	179
David Park, Musselburgh	61	57	61	179
Charlie Hunter, Prestwick	60	60	69	189

1873 ST ANDREWS

Tom Kidd, St Andrews	91	88	179
Jamie Anderson, St Andrews	91	89	180
Tom Morris Jr, St Andrews	94	89	183
Bob Kirk, Royal Blackheath	91	92	183
David Strath, St Andrews	97	90	187
Walter Gourlay, St Andrews	92	96	188

1874 MUSSELBURGH

Mungo Park, Musselburgh	75	84	159
Tom Morris Jr, St Andrews	83	78	161
George Paxton, Musselburgh	80	82	162
Bob Martin, St Andrews	85	79	164
Jamie Anderson, St Andrews	82	83	165
David Park, Musselburgh	83	83	166
W. Thomson, Edinburgh	84	82	166

1875 PRESTWICK

Willie Park, Musselburgh	56	59	51	166
Bob Martin, St Andrews	56	58	54	168
Mungo Park, Musselburgh	59	57	55	171
Robert Ferguson, Musselburgh	58	56	58	172
James Rennie, St Andrews	61	59	57	177
David Strath, St Andrews	59	61	58	178

1876 ST ANDREWS

Bob Martin, St Andrews	86	90	176
David Strath, North Berwick	86	90	176
(Martin was awarded the title when Strath refused to play-off)			
Willie Park, Musselburgh	94	89	183
Tom Morris Sr, St Andrews	90	95	185
W. Thomson, Elie	90	95	185
Mungo Park, Musselburgh	95	90	185

1877 MUSSELBURGH

Jamie Anderson, St Andrews	40	42	37	41	160
Bob Pringle, Musselburgh	44	38	40	40	162
Bob Ferguson, Musselburgh	40	40	40	44	164
William Cosgrove, Musselburgh	41	39	44	40	164
David Strath, North Berwick	45	40	38	43	166
William Brown, Musselburgh	39	41	45	41	166

1878 PRESTWICK

Jamie Anderson, St Andrews	53	53	51	157
Bob Kirk, St Andrews	53	55	51	159
J.O.F. Morris, St Andrews	50	56	55	161
Bob Martin, St Andrews	57	53	55	165
*John Ball, Hoylake	53	57	55	165
Willie Park, Musselburgh	53	56	57	166
William Cosgrove, Musselburgh	53	56	55	166

1879 ST ANDREWS

Jamie Anderson, St Andrews	84	85	169
James Allan, Westward Ho!	88	84	172
Andrew Kirkaldy, St Andrews	86	86	172
George Paxton, Musselburgh			174
Tom Kidd, St Andrews			175
Bob Ferguson, Musselburgh			176

1880 MUSSELBURGH

Bob Ferguson, Musselburgh	81	81	162
Peter Paxton, Musselburgh	81	86	167
Ned Cosgrove, Musselburgh	82	86	168
George Paxton, Musselburgh	85	84	169
Bob Pringle, Musselburgh	90	79	169
David Brown, Musselburgh	86	83	169

1881 PRESTWICK

Bob Ferguson, Musselburgh	53	60	57	170
Jamie Anderson, St Andrews	57	60	56	173
Ned Cosgrove, Musselburgh	61	59	57	177
Bob Martin, St Andrews	57	62	59	178
Tom Morris Sr, St Andrews	58	65	58	181
Willie Campbell, Musselburgh	60	56	65	181
Willie Park Jr, Musselburgh	66	57	58	181

1882 ST ANDREWS

Bob Ferguson, Musselburgh	83	88	171
Willie Fernie, Dumfries	88	86	174
Jamie Anderson, St Andrews	87	88	175
John Kirkaldy, St Andrews	86	89	175
Bob Martin, St Andrews	89	86	175
*Fitz Boothby, St Andrews	86	89	175

1883 MUSSELBURGH

Willie Fernie, Dumfries	75	84	159
Bob Ferguson, Musselburgh	78	80	159
(Fernie won play-off 158 to 159)			
Willie Brown, Musselburgh	83	77	160
Bob Pringle, Musselburgh	79	82	161
Willie Campbell, Musselburgh	80	83	163
George Paxton, Musselburgh	80	83	163

1884 PRESTWICK

Jack Simpson, Carnoustie	78	82	160
David Rollan, Elie	81	83	164
Willie Fernie, Felixstowe	80	84	164
Willie Campbell, Musselburgh	84	85	169
Willie Park Jr, Musselburgh	86	83	169
Ben Sayers, North Berwick	83	87	170

1885 ST ANDREWS

Bob Martin, St Andrews	84	87	171
Archie Simpson, Carnoustie	83	89	172
David Ayton, St Andrews	89	84	173
Willie Fernie, Felixstowe	89	85	174
Willie Park Jr, Musselburgh	86	88	174
Bob Simpson, Carnoustie	85	89	174

1886 MUSSELBURGH

David Brown, Musselburgh	79	78	157
Willie Campbell, Musselburgh	78	81	159
Ben Campbell, Musselburgh	79	81	160
Archie Simpson, Carnoustie	82	79	161
Willie Park Jr, Musselburgh	84	77	161
Thomas Gossett, Musselburgh	82	79	161
Bob Ferguson, Musselburgh	82	79	161

1887 PRESTWICK

Willie Park Jr, Musselburgh	82	79	161
Bob Martin, St Andrews	81	81	162
Willie Campbell, Prestwick	77	87	164
*Johnny Laidlay, Honourable Company	86	80	166
Ben Sayers, North Berwick	83	85	168
Archie Simpson, Carnoustie	81	87	168

1888 ST ANDREWS

Jack Burns, Warwick		86	85	171
David Anderson Jr, St Andrews		86	86	172
Ben Sayers, North Berwick		85	87	172
Willie Campbell, Prestwick		84	90	174
*Leslie Balfour, Edinburgh		86	89	175
Andrew Kirkaldy, St Andrews		87	89	176
David Grant, North Berwick		88	88	176

1889 MUSSELBURGH

Willie Park Jr, Musselburgh	39	39	39	38	155
Andrew Kirkaldy, St Andrews	39	38	39	39	155
(Park won play-off 158 to 163)					
Ben Sayes, North Berwick	39	40	41	39	159
*Johnny Laidlay, Honourable Company	42	39	40	41	162
David Brown, Musselburgh	43	39	41	39	162
Willie Fernie, Troon	45	39	40	40	164

1890 PRESTWICK

*John Ball, Royal Liverpool		82	82	164
Willie Fernie, Troon		85	82	167
Archie Simpson, Carnoustie		85	82	167
Willie Park Jr, Musselburgh		90	80	170
Andrew Kirkaldy, St Andrews		81	89	170
*Horace Hutchinson, Royal North Devon		87	85	172

1891 ST ANDREWS

Hugh Kirkaldy, St Andrews		83	83	166
Willie Fernie, Troon		84	84	168
Andrew Kirkaldy, St Andrews		84	84	168
S. Mure Fergusson, Royal and Ancient		86	84	170
W.D. More, Chester		84	87	171
Willie Park Jr, Musselburgh		88	85	173

(From 1892 the competition was extended to 72 holes)

1892 MUIRFIELD

*Harold Hilton, Royal Liverpool	78	81	72	74	305
*John Ball Jr, Royal Liverpool	75	80	74	79	308
James Kirkaldy, St Andrews	77	83	73	75	308
Sandy Herd, Huddersfield	77	78	77	76	308
J. Kay, Seaton Carew	82	78	74	78	312
Ben Sayers, North Berwick	80	76	81	75	312

1893 PRESTWICK

Willie Auchterlonie, St Andrews	78	81	81	82	322
*Johnny Laidlay, Honourable Company	80	83	80	81	324
Sandy Herd, Huddersfield	82	81	78	84	325
Hugh Kirkaldy, St Andrews	83	79	82	82	326
Andrew Kirkaldy, St Andrews	85	82	82	77	326
J. Kay, Seaton Carew	81	81	80	85	327
R. Simpson, Carnoustie	81	81	80	85	327

1894 SANDWICH

J.H. Taylor, Winchester	84	80	81	81	326
Douglas Rolland, Limpsfield	86	79	84	82	331
Andrew Kirkaldy, St Andrews	86	79	83	84	332
A. Toogood, Eltham	84	85	82	82	333
Willie Fernie, Troon	84	84	86	80	334
Harry Vardon, Bury St Edmunds	86	86	82	80	334
Ben Sayers, North Berwick	85	81	84	84	334

1895 ST ANDREWS

J.H. Taylor, Winchester	86	78	80	78	322
Sandy Herd, Huddersfield	82	77	82	85	326
Andrew Kirkaldy, St Andrews	81	83	84	84	332
G. Pulford, Hoylake	84	81	83	87	335
Archie Simpson, Aberdeen	88	85	78	85	336
Willie Fernie, Troon	86	79	86	86	337
David Brown, Malvern	81	89	83	84	337
David Anderson, Panmure	86	83	84	84	337

1896 MUIRFIELD

Harry Vardon, Ganton	83	78	78	77	316
J.H. Taylor, Winchester	77	78	81	80	316
(Vardon won play-off 157 to 161)					
*Freddie G. Tait, Black Watch	83	75	84	77	319
Willie Fernie, Troon	78	79	82	80	319
Sandy Herd, Huddersfield	72	84	79	85	320
James Braid, Romford	83	81	79	80	323

1897 HOYLAKE

*Harold H. Hilton, Royal Liverpool	80	75	84	75	314
James Braid, Romford	80	74	82	79	315
*Freddie G. Tait, Black Watch	79	79	80	79	317
G. Pulford, Hoylake	80	79	79	79	317
Sandy Herd, Huddersfield	78	81	79	80	318
Harry Vardon, Ganton	84	80	80	76	320

1898 PRESTWICK

Harry Vardon, Ganton	79	75	77	76	307
Willie Park, Musselburgh	76	75	78	79	308
*Harold H. Hilton, Royal Liverpool	76	81	77	75	309
J.H. Taylor, Winchester	78	78	77	79	312
*Freddie G. Tait, Black Watch	81	77	75	82	315
D. Kinnell, Leven	80	77	79	80	316

1899 SANDWICH

Harry Vardon, Ganton	76	76	81	77	310
Jack White, Seaford	79	79	82	75	315
Andrew Kirkaldy, St Andrews	81	79	82	77	319
J.H. Taylor, Mid-Surrey	77	76	83	84	320
James Braid, Romford	78	78	83	84	322
Willie Fernie, Troon	79	83	82	78	322

1900 ST ANDREWS

J.H. Taylor, Mid-Surrey	79	77	78	75	309
Harry Vardon, Ganton	79	81	80	78	317
James Braid, Romford	82	81	80	79	322
Jack White, Seaford	80	81	82	80	323

Willie Auchterlonie, St Andrews	81	85	80	80	326
Willie Park Jr, Musselburgh	80	83	81	84	328

1901 MUIRFIELD

James Braid, Romford	79	76	74	80	309
Harry Vardon, Ganton	77	78	79	78	312
J.H. Taylor, Mid-Surrey	79	83	74	77	313
*Harold H. Hilton, Royal Liverpool	89	80	75	76	320
Sandy Herd, Huddersfield	87	81	81	76	325
Jack White, Seaford	82	82	80	82	326

1902 HOYLAKE

Sandy Herd, Huddersfield	77	76	73	81	307
Harry Vardon, South Herts	72	77	80	79	308
James Braid, Walton Heath	78	76	80	74	308
R. Maxwell, Honourable Company	79	77	79	74	309
Tom Vardon, Ilkley	80	76	78	79	313
J.H. Taylor, Mid-Surrey	81	76	77	80	314
D. Kinnell, Leven	78	80	79	77	314
*Harold H. Hilton, Royal Liverpool	79	76	81	78	314

1903 PRESTWICK

Harry Vardon, South Herts	73	77	72	78	300
Tom Vardon, Ilkley	76	81	75	74	306
Jack White, Sunningdale	77	78	74	79	308
Sandy Herd, Huddersfield	73	83	76	77	309
James Braid, Walton Heath	77	79	79	75	310
R. Thompson, North Berwick	83	78	77	76	314
A.H. Scott, Elie	77	77	83	77	314

1904 SANDWICH

Jack White, Sunningdale	80	75	72	69	296
James Braid, Walton Heath	77	80	69	71	297
J.H. Taylor, Mid-Surrey	77	78	74	68	297
Tom Vardon, Ilkley	77	77	75	72	301
Harry Vardon, South Herts	76	73	79	74	302
James Sherlock, Stoke Poges	83	71	78	77	309

1905 ST ANDREWS

James Braid, Walton Heath	81	78	78	81	318
J.H. Taylor, Mid-Surrey	80	85	78	80	323
R. Jones, Wimbledon Park	81	77	87	78	323
J. Kinnell, Purley Downs	82	79	82	81	324
Arnaud Massy, La Boulie	81	80	82	82	325
E. Gray, Littlehampton	82	81	84	78	325

1906 MUIRFIELD

James Braid, Walton Heath	77	76	74	73	300
J.H. Taylor, Mid-Surrey	77	72	75	80	304
Harry Vardon, South Herts	77	73	77	78	305
*J. Graham Jr, Royal Liverpool	71	79	78	78	306
R. Jones, Wimbledon Park	74	78	73	83	308
Arnaud Massy, La Boulie	76	80	76	78	310

1907 HOYLAKE

Arnaud Massy, La Boulie	76	81	78	77	312
J.H. Taylor, Mid-Surrey	79	79	76	80	314

Tom Vardon, Sandwich	81	81	80	75	317
G. Pulford, Hoylake	81	78	80	78	317
Ted Ray, Ganton	83	80	79	76	318
James Braid, Walton Heath	82	85	75	76	318

1908 PRESTWICK

James Braid, Walton Heath	70	72	77	72	291
Tom Ball, West Lancashire	76	73	76	74	299
Ted Ray, Ganton	79	71	75	76	301
Sandy Herd, Huddersfield	74	74	79	75	302
Harry Vardon, South Herts	79	78	74	75	306
D. Kinnell, Prestwick St Nicholas	75	73	80	78	306

1909 DEAL

J.H. Taylor, Mid-Surrey	74	73	74	74	295
James Braid, Walton Heath	79	73	73	74	299
Tom Ball, West Lancashire	74	75	76	76	301
C. Johns, Southdown	72	76	79	75	302
T.G. Renouf, Manchester	76	78	76	73	303
Ted Ray, Ganton	77	76	76	75	304

1910 ST ANDREWS

James Braid, Walton Heath	76	73	74	76	299
Sandy Herd, Huddersfield	78	74	75	76	303
George Duncan, Hanger Hill	73	77	71	83	304
Laurie Ayton, Bishops Stortford	78	76	75	77	306
Ted Ray, Ganton	76	77	74	81	308
W. Smith, Mexico	77	71	80	80	308
J. Robson, West Surrey	75	80	77	76	308

1911 SANDWICH

Harry Vardon, South Herts	74	74	75	80	303
Arnaud Massy, St Jean de Luz	75	78	74	76	303
(Play-off; Massy conceded at the 35th hole)					
*Harold Hilton, Royal Liverpool	76	74	78	76	304
Sandy Herd, Coombe Hill	77	73	76	78	304
Ted Ray, Ganton	76	72	79	78	305
James Braid, Walton Heath	78	75	74	78	305
J.H. Taylor, Mid-Surrey	72	76	78	79	305

1912 MUIRFIELD

Ted Ray, Oxhey	71	73	76	75	295
Harry Vardon, South Herts	75	72	81	71	299
James Braid, Walton Heath	77	71	77	78	303
George Duncan, Hanger Hill	72	77	78	78	305
Laurie Ayton, Bishops Stortford	74	80	75	79	308
Sandy Herd, Coombe Hill	76	81	76	76	309

1913 HOYLAKE

J.H. Taylor, Mid-Surrey	73	75	77	79	304
Ted Ray, Oxhey	73	74	81	84	312
Harry Vardon, South Herts	79	75	79	80	313
M. Moran, Dollymount	76	74	89	74	313
Johnny J. McDermott, USA	75	80	77	83	315
T.G. Renouf, Manchester	75	78	84	78	315

1914 PRESTWICK

Harry Vardon, South Herts	73	77	78	78	306
J.H. Taylor, Mid-Surrey	74	78	74	83	309
H.B. Simpson, St Annes Old	77	80	78	75	310

Abe Mitchell, Sonning	76	78	79	79	312
Tom Williamson, Notts	75	79	79	79	312
R.G. Wilson, Croham Hurst	76	77	80	80	313

1920 DEAL

George Duncan, Hanger Hill	80	80	71	72	303
Sandy Herd, Coombe Hill	72	81	77	75	305
Ted Ray, Oxhey	72	83	78	73	306
Abe Mitchell, North Foreland	74	73	84	76	307
Len Holland, Northampton	80	78	71	79	308
Jim Barnes, USA	79	74	77	79	309

1921 ST ANDREWS

Jock Hutchison, USA	72	75	79	70	296
*Roger Wethered, Royal and Ancient	78	75	72	71	296
(Hutchison won play-off 150 to 159)					
T. Kerrigan, USA	74	80	72	72	298
Arthur G. Havers, West Lancs	76	74	77	72	299
George Duncan, Hanger Hill	74	75	78	74	301

1922 SANDWICH

Walter Hagen, USA	76	73	79	72	300
George Duncan, Hangar Hill	76	75	81	69	301
Jim Barnes, USA	75	76	77	73	301
Jock Hutchison, USA	79	74	73	76	302
Charles Whitcombe, Dorchester	77	79	72	75	303
J.H. Taylor, Mid-Surrey	73	78	76	77	304

1923 TROON

Arthur G. Havers, Coombe Hill	73	73	73	76	295
Walter Hagen, USA	76	71	74	75	296
Macdonald Smith, USA	80	73	69	75	297
Joe Kirkwood, Australia	72	79	69	78	298
Tom Fernie, Turnberry	73	78	74	75	300
George Duncan, Hanger Hill	79	75	74	74	302
Charles A. Whitcombe, Landsdowne	70	76	74	82	302

1924 HOYLAKE

Walter Hagen, USA	77	73	74	77	301
Ernest Whitcombe, Came Down	77	70	77	78	302
Macdonald Smith, USA	76	74	77	77	304
F. Ball, Langley Park	78	75	74	77	304
J.H. Taylor, Mid-Surrey	75	74	79	79	307
George Duncan, Hanger Hill	74	79	74	81	308
Aubrey Boomer, St Cloud, Paris	75	78	76	79	308

1925 PRESTWICK

Jim Barnes, USA	70	77	79	74	300
Archie Compston, North Manchester	76	75	75	75	301
Ted Ray, Oxhey	77	76	75	73	301
Macdonald Smith, USA	76	69	76	82	303
Abe Mitchell, Unattached	77	76	75	77	305

1926 ROYAL LYTHAM

*Robert T. Jones Jr, USA	72	72	73	74	291
Al Watrous, USA	71	75	69	78	293

Walter Hagen, USA	68	77	74	76	295
George von Elm, USA	75	72	76	72	295
Abe Mitchell, Unattached	78	78	72	71	299
T. Barber, Cavendish	77	73	78	71	299

1927 ST ANDREWS

*Robert T. Jones Jr, USA	68	72	73	72	285
Aubrey Boomer, St Cloud, Paris	76	70	73	72	291
Fred Robson, Cooden Beach	76	72	69	74	291
Joe Kirkwood, Australia	72	72	75	74	293
Ernest Whitcombe, Bournemouth	74	73	73	73	293
Charles Whitcombe, Crews Hill	74	76	71	75	296

1928 SANDWICH

Walter Hagen, USA	75	73	72	72	292
Gene Sarazen, USA	72	76	73	73	294
Archie Compston, Unattached	75	74	73	73	295
Percy Alliss, Berlin	75	76	75	72	298
Fred Robson, Cooden Beach	79	73	73	73	298
Jose Jurado, Argentina	74	71	76	80	301
Aubrey Boomer, St Cloud, Paris	79	73	77	72	301
Jim Barnes, USA	81	73	76	71	301

1929 MUIRFIELD

Walter Hagen, USA	75	67	75	75	292
John Farrell, USA	72	75	76	75	298
Leo Diegel, USA	71	69	82	77	299
Abe Mitchell, St Albans	72	72	78	78	300
Percy Alliss, Berlin	69	76	76	79	300
Bobby Cruickshank, USA	73	74	78	76	301

1930 HOYLAKE

*Robert T. Jones Jr, USA	70	72	74	75	291
Leo Diegel, USA	74	73	71	75	293
Macdonald Smith, USA	70	77	75	71	293
Fred Robson, Cooden Beach	71	72	78	75	296
Horton Smith, USA	72	73	78	73	296
Archie Compston, Coombe Hill	74	73	68	82	297
Jim Barnes, USA	71	77	72	77	297

1931 CARNOUSTIE

Tommy Armour, USA	73	75	77	71	296
Jose Jurado, Argentina	76	71	73	77	297
Percy Alliss, Berlin	74	78	73	73	298
Gene Sarazen, USA	74	76	75	73	298
Macdonald Smith, USA	75	77	71	76	299
John Farrell, USA	72	77	75	75	299

1932 PRINCE'S

Gene Sarazen, USA	70	69	70	74	283
Macdonald Smith, USA	71	76	71	70	288
Arthur G. Havers, Sandy Lodge	74	71	68	76	289
Charles Whitcombe, Crews Hill	71	73	73	75	292
Percy Alliss, Beaconsfield	71	71	78	72	292
Alf Padgham, Royal Ashdown Forest	76	72	74	70	292

1933 ST ANDREWS

Densmore Shute, USA	73	73	73	73	292
Craig Wood, USA	77	72	68	75	292
(Shute won play-off 149 to 154)					
Sid Easterbrook, Knowle	73	72	71	77	293
Gene Sarazen, USA	72	73	73	75	293
Leo Diegel, USA	75	70	71	77	293
Olin Dutra, USA	76	76	70	72	294

1934 SANDWICH

Henry Cotton, Waterloo, Belgium	67	65	72	79	283
Sid Brews, South Africa	76	71	70	71	288
Alf Padgham, Sundridge Park	71	70	75	74	290
Macdonald Smith, USA	77	71	72	72	292
Joe Kirkwood, USA	74	69	71	78	292
Marcel Dallemagne, France	71	73	71	77	292

1935 MUIRFIELD

Alf Perry, Leatherhead	69	75	67	72	283
Alf Padgham, Sundridge Park	70	72	74	71	287
Charles Whitcombe, Crews Hill	71	68	73	76	288
Bert Gadd, Brand Hall	72	75	71	71	289
Lawson Little, USA	75	71	74	69	289
Henry Picard, USA	72	73	72	75	292

1936 HOYLAKE

Alf Padgham, Sundridge Park	73	72	71	71	287
Jimmy Adams, Romford	71	73	71	73	288
Henry Cotton, Waterloo, Belgium	73	72	70	74	289
Marcel Dallemagne, France	73	72	75	69	289
Percy Alliss, Leeds Municipal	74	72	74	71	291
T. Green, Burnham Beeches	74	72	70	75	291
Gene Sarazen, USA	73	75	70	73	291

1937 CARNOUSTIE

Henry Cotton, Ashridge	74	72	73	71	290
Reg Whitcombe, Parkstone	72	70	74	76	292
Charles Lacey, USA	76	75	70	72	293
Charles Whitcombe, Crews Hill	73	71	74	76	294
Bryon Nelson, USA	75	76	71	74	296
Ed Dudley, USA	70	74	78	75	297

1938 SANDWICH

Reg Whitcombe, Parkstone	71	71	75	78	295
Jimmy Adams, Royal Liverpool	70	71	78	78	297
Henry Cotton, Ashridge	74	73	77	74	298
Alf Padgham, Sundridge Park	74	72	75	82	303
Jack Busson, Pannal	71	69	83	80	303
Richard Burton, Sale	71	69	78	85	303
Allan Dailey, Wanstead	73	72	80	78	303

1939 ST ANDREWS

Richard Burton, Sale	70	72	77	71	290
Johnny Bulla, USA	77	71	71	73	292
Johnny Fallon, Huddersfield	71	73	71	79	294
Bill Shankland, Temple Newsam	72	73	72	77	294
Alf Perry, Leatherhead	71	74	73	76	294

Reg Whitcombe, Parkstone	71	75	74	74	294
Sam King, Knole Park	74	72	75	73	294

1946 ST ANDREWS

Sam Snead, USA	71	70	74	75	290
Bobby Locke, South Africa	69	74	75	76	294
Johnny Bulla, USA	71	72	72	79	294
Charlie Ward, Little Aston	73	73	73	76	295
Henry Cotton, Royal Mid-Surrey	70	70	76	79	295
Dai Rees, Hindhead	75	67	73	80	295
Norman von Nida, Australia	70	76	74	75	295

1947 HOYLAKE

Fred Daly, Balmoral, Belfast	73	70	78	72	293
Reg Horne, Hendon	77	74	72	71	294
*Frank Stranahan, USA	71	79	72	72	294
Bill Shankland, Temple Newsam	76	74	75	70	295
Richard Burton, Coombe Hill	77	71	77	71	296
Charlie Ward, Little Aston	76	73	76	72	297
Sam King, Wildernesse	75	72	77	73	297
Arthur Lees, Dore and Totley	75	74	72	76	297
Johnny Bulla, USA	80	72	74	71	297
Henry Cotton, Royal Mid-Surrey	69	78	74	76	297
Norman von Nida, Australia	74	76	71	76	297

1948 MUIRFIELD

Henry Cotton, Royal Mid-Surrey	71	66	75	72	284
Fred Daly, Balmoral, Belfast	72	71	73	73	289
Norman von Nida, Australia	71	72	76	71	290
Roberto de Vicenzo, Argentina	70	73	72	75	290
Jack Hargreaves, Sutton Coldfield	76	68	73	73	290
Charlie Ward, Little Aston	69	72	75	74	290

1949 SANDWICH

Bobby Locke, South Africa	69	76	68	70	283
Harry Bradshaw, Kilcroney, Eire	68	77	68	70	283
(Locke won play-off 135 to 147)					
Roberto de Vicenzo, Argentina	68	75	73	69	285
Sam King, Knole Park	71	69	74	72	286
Charlie Ward, Little Aston	73	71	70	72	286
Arthur Lees, Dore and Totley	74	70	72	71	287
Max Faulkner, Royal Mid-Surrey	71	71	71	74	287

1950 TROON

Bobby Locke, South Africa	69	72	70	68	279
Roberto de Vicenzo, Argentina	72	71	68	70	281
Fred Daly, Balmoral, Belfast	75	72	69	66	282
Dai Rees, South Herts	71	68	72	71	282
E. Moore, South Africa	74	68	73	68	283
Max Faulkner, Royal Mid-Surrey	73	70	70	71	283

1951 ROYAL PORTRUSH

Max Faulkner, Unattached	71	70	70	74	285
Tony Cerda, Argentina	74	72	71	70	287
Charlie Ward, Little Aston	75	73	74	68	290
Fred Daly, Balmoral, Belfast	74	70	75	73	292
Jimmy Adams, Wentworth	68	77	75	72	292
Bobby Locke, South Africa	71	74	74	74	293

Bill Shankland, Temple Newsam	73	76	72	72	293
Norman Sutton, Leigh	73	70	74	76	293
Harry Weetman, Croham Hurst	73	71	75	74	293
Peter Thomson, Australia	70	75	73	75	293

1952 ROYAL LYTHAM

Bobby Locke, South Africa	69	71	74	73	287
Peter Thomson, Australia	68	73	77	70	288
Fred Daly, Balmoral, Belfast	67	69	77	76	289
Henry Cotton, Royal Mid-Surrey	75	74	74	71	294
Tony Cerda, Argentina	73	73	76	73	295
Sam King, Knole Park	71	74	74	76	295

1953 CARNOUSTIE

Ben Hogan, USA	73	71	70	68	282
*Frank Stranahan, USA	70	74	73	69	286
Dai Rees, South Herts	72	70	73	71	286
Peter Thomson, Australia	72	72	71	71	286
Tony Cerda, Argentina	75	71	69	71	286
Roberto de Vicenzo, Argentina	72	71	71	73	287

1954 ROYAL BIRKDALE

Peter Thomson, Australia	72	71	69	71	283
Sid Scott, Carlisle City	76	67	69	72	284
Dai Rees, South Herts	72	71	69	72	284
Bobby Locke, South Africa	74	71	69	70	284
Jimmy Adams, Royal Mid-Surrey	73	75	69	69	286
Tony Cerda, Argentina	71	71	73	71	286
J. Turnesa, USA	72	72	71	71	286

1955 ST ANDREWS

Peter Thomson, Australia	71	68	70	72	281
Johnny Fallon, Huddersfield	73	67	73	70	283
Frank Jowle, Edgbaston	70	71	69	74	284
Bobby Locke, South Africa	74	69	70	72	285
Tony Cerda, Argentina	73	71	71	71	286
Ken Bousfield, Coombe Hill	71	75	70	70	286
Harry Weetman, Croham Hurst	71	71	70	74	286
Bernard Hunt, Hartsbourne	70	71	74	71	286
Flory van Donck, Belgium	71	72	71	72	286

1956 HOYLAKE

Peter Thomson, Australia	70	70	72	74	286
Flory van Donck, Belgium	71	74	70	74	289
Roberto de Vicenzo, Argentina	71	70	79	70	290
Gary Player, South Africa	71	76	73	71	291
John Panton, Glenbervie	74	76	72	70	292
Henry Cotton, Temple	72	76	71	74	293
E. Bertolino, Argentina	69	72	76	76	293

1957 ST ANDREWS

Bobby Locke, South Africa	69	72	68	70	279
Peter Thomson, Australia	73	69	70	70	282
Eric Brown, Buchanan Castle	67	72	73	71	283
Angel Miguel, Spain	72	72	69	72	285
David Thomas, Sudbury	72	74	70	70	286
Tom Haliburton, Wentworth	72	73	68	73	286
*Dick Smith, Prestwick	71	72	72	71	286
Flory van Donck, Belgium	72	68	74	72	286

1958 ROYAL LYTHAM

Peter Thomson, Australia	66	72	67	73	278
David Thomas, Sudbury	70	68	69	71	278
(Thomson won play-off 139 to 143)					
Eric Brown, Buchanan Castle	73	70	65	71	279
Christy O'Connor, Killarney	67	68	73	71	279
Flory van Donck, Belgium	70	70	67	74	281
Leopoldo Ruiz, Argentina	71	65	72	73	281

1959 MUIRFIELD

Gary Player, South Africa	75	71	70	68	284
Flory van Donck, Belgium	70	70	73	73	286
Fred Bullock, Prestwick St Ninians	68	70	74	74	286
Sid Scott, Roehampton	73	70	73	71	287
Christy O'Connor, Royal Dublin	73	74	72	69	288
*Reid Jack, Dullatur	71	75	68	74	288
Sam King, Knole Park	70	74	68	76	288
John Panton, Glenbervie	72	72	71	73	288

1960 ST ANDREWS

Kel Nagle, Australia	69	67	71	71	278
Arnold Palmer, USA	70	71	70	68	279
Bernard Hunt, Hartsbourne	72	73	71	66	282
Harold Henning, South Africa	72	72	69	69	282
Roberto de Vicenzo, Argentina	67	67	75	73	282
*Guy Wolstenholme, Sunningdale	74	70	71	68	283

1961 ROYAL BIRKDALE

Arnold Palmer, USA	70	73	69	72	284
Dai Rees, South Herts	68	74	71	72	285
Christy O'Connor, Royal Dublin	71	77	67	73	288
Neil Coles, Coombe Hill	70	77	69	72	288
Eric Brown, Unattached	73	76	70	70	289
Kel Nagle, Australia	68	75	75	71	289

1962 TROON

Arnold Palmer, USA	71	69	67	69	276
Kel Nagle, Australia	71	71	70	70	282
Brian Huggett, Romford	75	71	74	69	289
Phil Rodgers, USA	75	70	72	72	289
Bob Charles, NZ	75	70	70	75	290
Sam Snead, USA	76	73	72	71	292
Peter Thomson, Australia	70	77	75	70	292

1963 ROYAL LYTHAM

Bob Charles, NZ	68	72	66	71	277
Phil Rodgers, USA	67	68	73	69	277
(Charles won play-off 140 to 148)					
Jack Nicklaus, USA	71	67	70	70	278
Kel Nagle, Australia	69	70	73	71	283
Peter Thomson, Australia	67	69	71	78	285
Christy O'Connor, Royal Dublin	74	68	76	68	286

1964 ST ANDREWS

Tony Lema, USA	73	68	68	70	279
Jack Nicklaus, USA	76	74	66	68	284
Roberto de Vicenzo, Argentina	76	72	70	67	285

Bernard Hunt, Hartsbourne	73	74	70	70	287
Bruce Devlin, Australia	72	72	73	73	290
Christy O'Connor, Royal Dublin	71	73	74	73	291
Harry Weetman, Selsdon Park	72	71	75	73	291

1965 ROYAL BIRKDALE

Peter Thomson, Australia	74	68	72	71	285
Christy O'Connor, Royal Dublin	69	73	74	71	287
Brian Huggett, Romford	73	68	76	70	287
Roberto de Vicenzo, Argentina	74	69	73	72	288
Kel Nagle, Australia	74	70	73	72	289
Tony Lema, USA	68	72	75	74	289
Bernard Hunt, Hartsbourne	74	74	70	71	289

1966 MUIRFIELD

Jack Nicklaus, USA	70	67	75	70	282
David Thomas, Dunham Forest	72	73	69	69	283
Doug Sanders, USA	71	70	72	70	283
Gary Player, South Africa	72	74	71	69	286
Bruce Devlin, Australia	73	69	74	70	286
Kel Nagle, Australia	72	68	76	70	286
Phil Rodgers, USA	74	66	70	76	286

1967 HOYLAKE

Roberto de Vicenzo, Argentina	70	71	67	70	278
Jack Nicklaus, USA	71	69	71	69	280
Clive Clark, Sunningdale	70	73	69	72	284
Gary Player, South Africa	72	71	67	74	284
Tony Jacklin, Potters Bar	73	69	73	70	285
Sebastian Miguel, Spain	72	74	68	72	286
Harold Henning, South Africa	74	70	71	71	286

1968 CARNOUSTIE

Gary Player, South Africa	74	71	71	73	289
Jack Nicklaus, USA	76	69	73	73	291
Bob Charles, NZ	72	72	71	76	291
Billy Casper, USA	72	68	74	78	292
Maurice Bembridge, Little Aston	71	75	73	74	293
Brian Barnes, Burnham & Berrow	70	74	80	71	295
Neil Coles, Coombe Hill	75	76	71	73	295
Gay Brewer, USA	74	73	72	76	295

1969 ROYAL LYTHAM

Tony Jacklin, Potters Bar	68	70	70	72	280
Bob Charles, NZ	66	69	75	72	282
Peter Thomson, Australia	71	70	70	72	283
Roberto de Vicenzo, Argentina	72	73	66	72	283
Christy O'Connor, Royal Dublin	71	65	74	74	284
Jack Nicklaus, USA	75	70	68	72	285
Davis Love Jr, USA	70	73	71	71	285

1970 ST ANDREWS

Jack Nicklaus, USA	68	69	73	73	283
Doug Sanders, USA	68	71	71	73	283
(Nicklaus won play-off 72 to 73)					
Harold Henning, South Africa	67	72	73	73	285
Lee Trevino, USA	68	68	72	77	285
Tony Jacklin, Potters Bar	67	70	73	76	286
Neil Coles, Coombe Hill	65	74	72	76	287

Peter Oosterhuis, Dulwich and Sydenham	73	69	69	76	287

1971 ROYAL BIRKDALE

Lee Trevino, USA	69	70	69	70	278
Lu Liang Huan, Taiwan	70	70	69	70	279
Tony Jacklin, Potters Bar	69	70	70	71	280
Craig de Foy, Coombe Hill	72	72	68	69	281
Jack Nicklaus, USA	71	71	72	69	283
Charles Coody, USA	74	71	70	68	283

1972 MUIRFIELD

Lee Trevino, USA	71	70	66	71	278
Jack Nicklaus, USA	70	72	71	66	279
Tony Jacklin, Potters Bar	69	72	67	72	280
Doug Sanders, USA	71	71	69	70	281
Brian Barnes, Fairway DR	71	72	69	71	283
Gary Player, South Africa	71	71	76	67	285

1973 TROON

Tom Weiskopf, USA	68	67	71	70	276
Neil Coles, Holiday Inns	71	72	70	66	279
Johnny Miller, USA	70	68	69	72	279
Jack Nicklaus, USA	69	70	76	65	280
Bert Yancey, USA	69	69	73	70	281
Peter Butler, Golf Domes	71	72	74	69	286

1974 ROYAL LYTHAM

Gary Player, South Africa	69	68	75	70	282
Peter Oosterhuis, Pacific Harbour	71	71	73	71	286
Jack Nicklaus, USA	74	72	70	71	287
Hubert Green, USA	71	74	72	71	288
Danny Edwards, USA	70	73	76	73	292
Lu Liang Huan, Taiwan	72	72	75	73	292

1975 CARNOUSTIE

Tom Watson, USA	71	67	69	72	279
Jack Newton, Australia	69	71	65	74	279
(Watson won play-off 71 to 72)					
Bobby Cole, South Africa	72	66	66	76	280
Jack Nicklaus, USA	69	71	68	72	280
Johnny Miller, USA	71	69	66	74	280
Graham Marsh, Australia	72	67	71	71	281

1976 ROYAL BIRKDALE

Johnny Miller, USA	72	68	73	66	279
Jack Nicklaus, USA	74	70	72	69	285
Severiano Ballesteros, Spain	69	69	73	74	285
Raymond Floyd, USA	76	67	73	70	286
Mark James, Burghley Park	76	72	74	66	288
Hubert Green, USA	72	70	78	68	288
Christy O'Connor Jr, Shannon	69	73	75	71	288
Tom Kite, USA	70	74	73	71	288
Tommy Horton, Royal Jersey	74	69	72	73	288

1977 TURNBERRY

Tom Watson, USA	68	70	65	65	268
Jack Nicklaus, USA	68	70	65	66	269

Hubert Green, USA	72	66	74	67	279
Lee Trevino, USA	68	70	72	70	280
Ben Crenshaw, USA	71	69	66	75	281
George Burns, USA	70	70	72	69	281

1978 ST ANDREWS

Jack Nicklaus, USA	71	72	69	69	281
Simon Owen, NZ	70	75	67	71	283
Ben Crenshaw, USA	70	69	73	71	283
Raymond Floyd, USA	69	75	71	68	283
Tom Kite, USA	72	69	72	70	283
Peter Oosterhuis, GB	72	70	69	73	284

1979 ROYAL LYTHAM

Severiano Ballesteros, Spain	73	65	75	70	283
Jack Nicklaus, USA	72	69	73	72	286
Ben Crenshaw, USA	72	71	72	71	286
Mark James, Burghley Park	76	69	69	73	287
Rodger Davis, Australia	75	70	70	73	288
Hale Irwin, USA	68	68	75	78	289

1980 MUIRFIELD

Tom Watson, USA	68	70	64	69	271
Lee Trevino, USA	68	67	71	69	275
Ben Crenshaw, USA	70	70	68	69	277
Jack Nicklaus, USA	73	67	71	69	280
Carl Mason, Unattached	72	69	70	69	280

1981 SANDWICH

Bill Rogers, USA	72	66	67	71	276
Bernhard Langer, Germany	73	67	70	70	280
Mark James, Otley	72	70	68	73	283
Raymond Floyd, USA	74	70	69	70	283
Sam Torrance, Caledonian Hotel	72	69	73	70	284
Bruce Leitzke, USA	76	69	71	69	285
Manuel Pinero, Spain	73	74	68	70	285

1982 TROON

Tom Watson, USA	69	71	74	70	284
Peter Oosterhuis, GB	74	67	74	70	285
Nick Price, South Africa	69	69	74	73	285
Nick Faldo, Glynwed Ltd	73	73	71	69	286
Des Smyth, EAL Tubes	70	69	74	73	286
Tom Purtzer, USA	76	66	75	69	286
Massy Kuramoto, Japan	71	73	71	71	286

1983 ROYAL BIRKDALE

Tom Watson, USA	67	68	70	70	275
Hale Irwin, USA	69	68	72	67	276
Andy Bean, USA	70	69	70	67	276
Graham Marsh, Australia	69	70	74	64	277
Lee Trevino, USA	69	66	73	70	278
Severiano Ballesteros, Spain	71	71	69	68	279
Harold Henning, South Africa	71	69	70	69	279

1984 ST ANDREWS

Severiano Ballesteros, Spain	69	68	70	69	276
Bernhard Langer, Germany	71	68	68	71	278
Tom Watson, USA	71	68	66	73	278
Fred Couples, USA	70	69	74	68	281

Lanny Wadkins, USA	70	69	73	69	281
Greg Norman, Australia	67	74	74	67	282
Nick Faldo, Glynwed Int.	69	68	76	69	282

1985 SANDWICH

Sandy Lyle, Scotland	68	71	73	70	282
Payne Stewart, USA	70	75	70	68	283
Jose Rivero, Spain	74	72	70	68	284
Christy O'Connor Jr, Ireland	64	76	72	72	284
Mark O'Meara, USA	70	72	70	72	284
David Graham, Australia	68	71	70	75	284
Bernhard Langer, Germany	72	69	68	75	284

1986 TURNBERRY

Greg Norman, Australia	74	63	74	69	280
Gordon J. Brand, England	71	68	75	71	285
Bernhard Langer, Germany	72	70	76	68	286
Ian Woosnam, Wales	70	74	70	72	286
Nick Faldo, England	71	70	76	70	287

1987 MUIRFIELD

Nick Faldo, England	68	69	71	71	279
Rodger Davis, Australia	64	73	74	69	280
Paul Azinger, USA	68	68	71	73	280
Ben Crenshaw, USA	73	68	72	68	281
Payne Stewart, USA	71	66	72	72	281
David Frost, South Africa	70	68	70	74	282
Tom Watson, USA	69	69	71	74	283

1988 ROYAL LYTHAM

Severiano Ballesteros, Spain	67	71	70	65	273
Nick Price, Zimbabwe	70	67	69	69	275
Nick Faldo, England	71	69	68	71	279
Fred Couples, USA	73	69	71	68	281
Gary Koch, USA	71	72	70	68	281
Peter Senior, Australia	70	73	70	69	282

1989 ROYAL TROON

Mark Calcavecchia, USA	71	68	68	68	275
Greg Norman, Australia	69	70	72	64	275
Wayne Grady, Australia	68	67	69	71	275
(Calcavecchia won four-hole play-off)					
Tom Watson, USA	69	68	68	72	277
Jodie Mudd, USA	73	67	68	70	278

1990 ST ANDREWS

Nick Faldo, England	67	65	67	71	270
Mark McNulty, Zimbabwe	74	68	68	65	275
Payne Stewart, USA	68	68	68	71	275
Jodie Mudd, USA	72	66	72	66	276
Ian Woosnam, Wales	68	69	70	69	276

1991 ROYAL BIRKDALE

Ian Baker-Finch, Australia	71	71	64	66	272
Mike Harwood, Australia	68	70	69	67	274
Fred Couples, USA	72	69	70	64	275
Mark O'Meara, USA	71	68	67	69	275
Jodie Mudd, USA	72	70	72	63	277
Bob Tway, USA	75	66	70	66	277
Eamonn Darcy, Ireland	73	68	66	70	277

FINAL RESULTS

HOLE		1	2	3	4	5	6	7	8	9	10	11	12	13	14	15	16	17	18	
PAR		4	4	4	3	5	4	3	4	5	4	4	4	3	4	4	3	5	4	TOTAL
Nick Faldo	Round 1	5	4	4	3	3	4	3	3	4	3	4	4	2	4	4	3	5	4	66
	Round 2	4	4	4	3	4	3	4	4	3	3	4	3	3	3	3	3	5	4	64
	Round 3	4	4	4	2	5	4	3	4	5	5	4	3	3	4	4	3	4	4	69
	Round 4	5	4	4	3	5	4	3	4	5	4	5	4	4	5	3	3	4	4	73-272
John Cook	Round 1	3	4	3	3	4	4	3	4	4	5	4	4	3	4	4	3	3	4	66
	Round 2	4	4	4	3	3	3	3	3	5	4	3	5	4	4	4	3	4	4	67
	Round 3	5	4	4	3	4	4	4	4	3	4	4	4	3	5	4	3	4	4	70
	Round 4	5	4	3	3	3	4	4	4	7	4	4	3	3	4	3	2	5	5	70-273
Jose Maria Olazabal	Round 1	4	4	4	3	4	4	3	4	5	4	4	5	2	4	4	3	5	4	70
	Round 2	5	4	3	3	4	4	3	4	4	3	3	5	2	4	4	3	5	4	67
	Round 3	4	5	4	4	4	4	3	5	4	4	4	3	3	4	4	3	3	4	69
	Round 4	5	3	4	4	5	4	3	4	4	3	3	3	3	4	4	3	4	4	68-274
Steve Pate	Round 1	4	4	4	3	4	3	3	4	4	4	4	4	2	3	3	3	4	4	64
	Round 2	4	4	3	3	5	4	2	3	5	4	4	4	4	5	3	3	5	5	70
	Round 3	4	4	3	2	4	3	4	4	6	4	3	3	3	5	5	3	4	5	69
	Round 4	4	5	3	4	4	3	3	4	6	4	4	4	3	5	6	3	4	4	73-276
Andrew Magee	Round 1	5	4	4	2	4	4	3	4	5	4	4	4	2	4	3	3	4	4	67
	Round 2	4	5	4	3	4	4	2	4	5	5	5	3	3	4	4	3	5	5	72
	Round 3	4	4	4	3	5	4	3	5	4	4	3	4	3	5	4	3	4	4	70
	Round 4	4	4	4	3	3	4	3	4	4	4	4	4	3	5	4	3	5	5	70-279
Malcolm Mackenzie	Round 1	4	4	3	4	4	3	3	4	5	4	3	4	3	5	5	4	5	4	71
	Round 2	4	3	4	2	4	4	3	4	4	4	4	4	3	4	4	3	5	4	67
	Round 3	5	5	3	4	4	3	3	4	5	4	3	4	2	4	4	3	4	5	70
	Round 4	4	4	5	2	4	4	4	4	4	4	5	4	3	4	4	4	4	4	71-279
Robert Karlsson	Round 1	5	4	4	3	5	4	4	3	5	3	4	4	2	4	4	3	4	5	70
	Round 2	4	3	4	3	4	3	3	4	4	5	4	4	3	5	4	3	4	4	68
	Round 3	3	4	3	2	5	5	3	4	4	5	4	4	3	4	4	5	5	4	70
	Round 4	5	4	4	3	5	4	3	4	7	4	4	2	2	4	4	2	4	4	71-279
Ian Woosnam	Round 1	4	3	4	3	4	4	3	3	4	3	4	4	3	3	3	3	5	5	65
	Round 2	4	4	4	4	4	5	3	4	5	5	4	4	2	5	5	4	4	4	73
	Round 3	4	3	4	2	5	6	5	5	4	4	3	3	3	4	4	3	4	4	70
	Round 4	4	4	4	3	5	5	4	4	5	3	4	4	3	5	4	2	4	4	71-279
Gordon Brand, Jr.	Round 1	4	3	4	2	4	4	3	3	5	3	4	4	3	4	4	3	4	4	65
	Round 2	5	4	4	3	4	4	3	4	5	3	4	4	2	3	4	3	5	4	68
	Round 3	4	4	4	3	4	4	3	4	4	4	4	5	3	6	5	3	4	4	72
	Round 4	4	4	4	4	4	5	3	4	5	4	4	5	2	5	5	5	4	3	74-279
Donnie Hammond	Round 1	4	4	4	3	4	5	3	4	5	3	4	4	3	4	5	3	4	4	70
	Round 2	4	4	3	2	5	5	2	3	4	4	4	3	3	5	4	3	3	4	65
	Round 3	5	3	4	3	4	4	3	4	4	4	4	4	3	5	5	2	4	5	70
	Round 4	3	5	3	3	5	5	3	4	6	5	5	4	3	4	4	4	4	4	74-279
Ernie Els	Round 1	4	4	4	3	4	4	3	3	5	4	3	5	2	4	4	3	4	3	66
	Round 2	4	3	3	3	5	5	3	4	5	4	3	4	3	4	4	3	4	5	69
	Round 3	4	4	4	4	4	4	3	4	5	4	4	4	3	4	4	3	4	4	70
	Round 4	5	5	4	3	6	3	4	4	6	4	3	4	3	5	3	3	4	5	74-279

Former Ryder Cup player Ken Brown (left) and Japanese star Isao Aoki were radio and television commentators.

A perk of the job, television cameramen have the best views of the course.

The world's Press always gathers in large numbers for the Open Championship.